Vol. VI

No. 2

Home Study
Large-Print Edition

SPRING QUARTER   March, April, May 2023

Editor in Chief: Kenneth Sponsler

Union Gospel Press

Edited and published quarterly by
THE INCORPORATED TRUSTEES OF THE
GOSPEL WORKER SOCIETY
UNION GOSPEL PRESS DIVISION

Rev. W. B. Musselman, Founder

Price: $4.99 per quarter*
shipping and handling extra

ISBN 978-1-64495-323-5

HOW TO PLEASE THE FATHER

DON RUFF

God the Father has done so much for His people that it is hard to know where to begin to thank Him. James 1:17 says, "Every good gift and every perfect gift is from above, and cometh down from the Father of lights." In gratitude for all He does, what can Christians do to please Him?

Looking at the life and ministry of Jesus Christ can help give an answer to that question. Jesus pleased the Father in every way. The lessons this quarter focus on this theme. He pleased the Father through His works, His sacrifice, and His teachings.

Before beginning His great ministry, Jesus needed to be introduced to His forerunner and to those around him. John the Baptist declared that the Messiah had come. John's baptism was a call to repentance, and the sinless Jesus had come to identify with sinners and later become sin for all when He died on the cross. The Father declared His pleasure with His Son as the Spirit descended on Jesus.

Believers identify with Christ when they are baptized. Baptism shows the world that a person has made a decision to put away the desire to sin and to commit to Christian service. With that big step, the Father is pleased when someone who has trusted in Jesus as Saviour then professes Him before others through baptism.

After Jesus was baptized, the Spirit led Him into a desert area to be tested by Satan. Satan tempted Him with the lust of the flesh, the pride of life, and the lust of the eyes. Jesus was tempted in every way that mere humans are tempted so that He could again identify with His creation. Since He did not give in, He was the perfect Sacrifice for our sins and the perfect Mediator between all believers and the Holy God. Jesus pleased the Father by denying Himself the pleasures offered by Satan and sin, so Jesus knows what it is like to suffer and to be tempted.

His example is for Christians to follow. Pleasing the Father means committing to trusting in His power that enables us to resist the temptation to sin. (Remember that temptation is not sin. Giving in to temptation is sin.) The Father gives the needed strength through studying and memorizing His Word. Each Christian should respond to temptation with Scripture as Jesus did.

Throughout His earthly ministry, Jesus pleased His Father by giving Him glory and doing what He had sent Him to do. Jesus said that He would do only those things the Father would have Him do (cf. John 5:19). The Father sent the Son into the world to reveal His love, grace, mercy, holiness, power, and so much more to His fallen creation.

Those who belong to the Father are part of that same great enterprise. Each believer has the responsibility and privilege to shine the light of His love to others. It pleases the Father when His children tell others about the salvation found in Christ. Just as Jesus said that it

PLEASE NOTE: Fundamental, sound doctrine is the objective of The Incorporated Trustees of the Gospel Worker Society, Union Gospel Press Division. The writers are prayerfully selected for their Bible knowledge and yieldedness to the Spirit of Truth, each writing in his own style as enlightened by the Holy Spirit. At best we know in part only. "They received the word with all readiness of mind, and searched the scriptures daily, whether those things were so" (Acts 17:11).

is only natural for Him, the Son, to show forth the Father, it is also only natural for believers to do the same for the Lord.

Jesus set the ultimate example of pleasing the Father when He faced the terrible ordeal of arrest, unjust trials, scourging, and death by crucifixion. He knew beforehand how terrible it would be to experience all those things, so He prepared Himself through prayer. During that prayer, we see how at first, He asked His Father if it was possible not to have to endure the forthcoming torture, abandonment, and death. Despite all that He knew was coming, Jesus pleased the Father by trusting and submitting to His will. He died for the sins of the world to please the Holy Father's requirement for atonement.

Jesus sought God's will and strength to endure being our Sacrifice for sin. Believers can follow His example. They can "die daily" (I Cor. 15:31) to sin, the flesh, and self (Rom. 6:11; Gal. 2:20; 5:24). This is how believers imitate Christ and please the Father. The things of this world will constantly contend for His children's attention, but "dying daily" to self can help conquer sin.

The Father validated the work of the Son when He raised Him from the dead. Christ had indeed been dead for three days in the tomb, but the Father was pleased by His sacrifice and raised the Son from the dead to guarantee victory over sin and death (Gal. 1:1). Christ gave proofs of who He is. Without the resurrection, Jesus would not have power over the grave.

We must accept Jesus' resurrection as fact to have eternal life (Rom. 10:8-9). We please the Father, and He sanctifies us by His grace through faith in Christ's death and resurrection.

During His earthly ministry, Jesus pleased the Father through His teachings. He taught His disciples about the Father, the Spirit, and Himself. He pointed out the truths God wanted them to know and believe. Jesus told

His followers that He is the Bread of Life, the Light of the World, the Good Shepherd, and the True Vine. Those truths can lead the lost to salvation in Christ the Son. He fulfilled Old Testament prophecies about Himself (Ex. 16; Ps. 118:20; Isa. 5:1-7).

Christians can please the Father by learning His truths. Those truths can be passed on to believers to encourage them through the trials of life. The lost need to hear those truths.

God is pleased with prayer. Jesus prayed fervently and habitually to the Father, showing His dependence on Him. Jesus always prayed for His followers, and He sits at the right of the Father interceding for Christians.

Christians can please the Father by praying for others just as Jesus did. His Word instructs believers to pray at all times for one another (Eph. 6:18).

While Jesus was on earth, He did not seek to live for Himself. He sought to please the Father in all things. He was focused on the mission the Father had sent Him to complete. Jesus sought the will of God to build His kingdom. Believers are to follow Christ's example.

SCRIPTURE LESSON TEXT

MARK 1:4 John did baptize in the wilderness, and preach the baptism of repentance for the remission of sins.

5 And there went out unto him all the land of Judaea, and they of Jerusalem, and were all baptized of him in the river of Jordan, confessing their sins.

6 And John was clothed with camel's hair, and with a girdle of a skin about his loins; and he did eat locusts and wild honey;

7 And preached, saying, There cometh one mightier than I after me, the latchet of whose shoes I am not worthy to stoop down and unloose.

8 I indeed have baptized you with water: but he shall baptize you with the Holy Ghost.

9 And it came to pass in those days, that Jesus came from Nazareth of Galilee, and was baptized of John in Jordan.

10 And straightway coming up out of the water, he saw the heavens opened, and the Spirit like a dove descending upon him:

11 And there came a voice from heaven, *saying,* Thou art my beloved Son, in whom I am well pleased.

12 And immediately the Spirit driveth him into the wilderness.

13 And he was there in the wilderness forty days, tempted of Satan; and was with the wild beasts; and the angels ministered unto him.

NOTES

Jesus' Baptism

Lesson Text: Mark 1:4-13

Related Scriptures: Matthew 3:1-17; Luke 3:15-22;
Matthew 17:1-7; Mark 9:2-8; Luke 9:28-36

TIME: A.D. 26   PLACES: wilderness of Judea; Jordan River

GOLDEN TEXT—"There came a voice from heaven, saying, Thou art my beloved Son, in whom I am well pleased" (Mark 1:11).

Lesson Exposition

People love to ask successful entrepreneurs, "How did you start your business? How did you begin your career?" We like to know the secret behind the apparent good circumstances of our community leaders. Beginnings are important, for they set the tone for what is to follow. Sometimes we make several false starts before we discover our mission in life.

When Jesus was growing up in Nazareth, He had a long time to think about His leadership role in God's redemptive plan. Then, when Jesus acted, there was no doubt that He knew what He was doing. His first experience was somewhat humbling (namely, being baptized by John), and His second experience was quite probing (namely, being tempted by Satan). In each and every situation, the Son knew that the Father had sent Him.

THE MINISTRY OF JOHN—
Mark 1:4-8

The arrival of John (Mark 1:4). At the outset of Mark's written work, he stated that his Gospel was about Jesus (vs. 1); yet the first person Mark presented in his account was not Jesus but John the Baptist (vss. 2-8). That may seem odd; however, in Mark's view, the gospel of Jesus had its beginning in the ministry of John.

John's birth (around 5 B.C.) came about because of a special intervention of the Lord. Both Zacharias and Elisabeth, his parents, were godly people, but they were old and had no children. That is why Zacharias, a priest, was astounded when he received God's message about a son to be born. As a result, the angel made him speechless until John was born (Luke 1:5-22, 57-66).

It was about A.D. 26, when he was about thirty-one years old, that John started to preach in the wilderness. God used this prophet in the desert to summon the people of his day to repent and be baptized (Mark 1:4). Repentance was necessary because God's kingdom, in the Person of Christ, was close at hand. Repentance means a change in behavior. John was looking for deep and lasting change. Repentant sinners acknowledged that they had broken God's laws and that they deserved His judgment.

In Bible times, there were no superhighways. When an important dignitary was expected to travel through the country, a messenger would go out in advance to tell the people to prepare the way for the dignitary's coming. This meant they had to improve roads by cutting down trees, leveling steep hills, and generally clearing away obstacles. Figuratively speaking, this was the ministry of John. He was a messenger preparing the hearts of people for the coming Messiah (cf. Isa. 40:3; Mal. 3:1).

The response of the crowd to John (Mark 1:5-6). John was not the kind of person one might expect to get the job of Messiah's forerunner. As far as we know, John never served as a priest, even though he was born into a priestly family; nor did he serve as a scribe. He was neither a Pharisee nor a Sadducee. John avoided cities, taking his message into the wilderness instead.

This region is a dry, hilly, barren territory between Jerusalem and the Jordan River, overlooking the Dead Sea. One oasis in the desert is the city of Jericho. This was probably where John first preached for two reasons: it was the main center for travelers from all over the East, and it was close to the river. When the people in Jericho heard the Lord's herald, the news spread quickly to Jerusalem and all Judea (vs. 5).

In those days, non-Jews who wanted to make Judaism their religion were baptized as a symbol of spiritual cleansing. The Jews themselves, however, were not used to hearing that they needed to be baptized to be made righteous for the coming Messiah.

People in our day have some of the same hesitations about repentance that John's contemporaries must have had. It can seem embarrassing to admit that we need to change, yet it is only the humble who receive God's forgiveness.

The baptism that people underwent in the Jordan River signified that they had turned from their sins and turned to God to be forgiven. Their willingness to confess their misdeeds harmonized with this decision.

John was eccentric in his dress and behavior. He wore a garment of camel hair that he tied at his waist with a leather strap. This outfit made him similar in appearance to Elijah the prophet (cf. II Kgs. 1:8). John's food included locusts and wild honey, which were common in desert regions. John's lifestyle was in stark contrast to that of many of the religious leaders of Jerusalem, who lived in relative ease and luxury.

The message of John (Mark 1:7-8). Even with all his popularity, John knew Christ was infinitely superior to him. John expressed Christ's superior status by declaring his own unworthiness to untie Jesus' sandals, a task inevitably followed by washing the feet. John shrank from assuming the position of even the lowliest servant to Christ. John was Christ's forerunner, not His competitor.

John declared that he offered a symbol (water) that held no real power to cleanse sin. In contrast, Jesus would baptize with the Holy Spirit, providing an actual cleansing from sin (vs. 8). In addition, the Spirit signified the permanent dwelling of God in believers (John 14:16-17; I Cor. 6:19). According to Matthew 3:11, John additionally noted that Jesus would baptize with fire.

THE SAVIOUR'S BAPTISM AND TEMPTATION—Mark 1:9-13

The Saviour's baptism (Mark 1:9-11). The climax of John's ministry came when he baptized Jesus. One day, perhaps while John was preoccupied with his work, Jesus traveled south from His hometown of Nazareth in Galilee and arrived at the spot where John was ministering. The Saviour then had John baptize Him.

Three reasons for this incident are worth mentioning. First, Jesus wished to identify with sinners. He especially wanted to associate with those who hungered for righteousness. Second, Jesus sought to represent sinners. He was baptized as the Representative of all people. In this way, He demonstrated that everyone needs to repent, for all people need cleansing from sin. Third, Jesus' baptism foreshadowed His own death, burial, and resurrection for sinners (Rom. 6:3-4).

As Jesus came out of the water, God publicly affirmed Him in two ways (Mark 1:10-11). First, the Holy Spirit descended upon the Son in the likeness of a dove. This visible anointing revealed that Jesus is the Messiah. Second, the Father audibly identified and endorsed Jesus. In a sense, the entire Trinity was involved. The initiative of the Father, the atoning work of the Son, and enabling power of the Spirit were present together.

The Saviour's temptation (Mark 1:12-13). Immediately after Jesus' baptism, the Spirit sent Him into the desert, where He became the object of Satan's personal assaults. This was no task for a lesser demon. If the Son of God were to be drawn away from obedience to the Father's will, it would require the most diabolical efforts from the prince of darkness himself. Satan thus assaulted Jesus with his worst— but without success. Jesus emerged triumphant. Afterward, angels ministered to Him, likely with nourishment, comfort, and protection.

While Matthew and Luke also mentioned Jesus' temptation in the wilderness for forty days (Matt. 4:1-11; Luke 4:1-13), only Mark mentioned the presence of wild animals (Mark 1:13). One reason may be that Mark wanted to emphasize the danger Jesus faced. In Jesus' day, far more wild animals roamed the countryside than today, including lions that prowled the wooded areas along the Jordan River (Jer. 5:6; 49:19).

Another reason for mentioning wild animals may be that untamed beasts were associated with evil powers. The historical episode, in a sense, became a symbol of the cosmic struggle of good and evil in which Jesus was engaged. In addition, the wild beasts might be connected to the hope of the messianic era, when animal enemies such as the wolf and the lamb will live in peace (Isa. 11:6-9).

A third reason may come from Mark's audience. If Mark was writing his Gospel for Gentile Christians sometime between A.D. 60 and 70 and particularly for those in Rome (cf. I Pet. 5:13), they would be facing persecutions from Nero that often included being thrown to the lions for refusing to worship the emperor. The early Christians could take comfort in the fact that Jesus too had confronted wild animals.

—Dan Lioy.

PRACTICAL POINTS

1. The starting point for a relationship with the Messiah is genuine repentance from sins (Mark 1:4).

2. Part of the process of turning to faith in the Saviour involves acknowledging our misdeeds (vs. 5).

3. None of us is so unique and distinctive that he cannot allow the Lord to take first place in his life (vss. 6-8).

4. Our Lord was willing to humble Himself on our behalf so that we could be saved (vs. 9).

5. Unlike the religious frauds who have made false claims to be the Messiah down through the centuries, Jesus truly is the Saviour of the world (vss. 10-11).

6. During His time on earth, Jesus experienced real temptations and always triumphed over them through the presence and power of the Holy Spirit (vss. 12-13).

—Dan Lioy.

FOR DAILY MEDITATION

MONDAY, Feb. 27.   Luke 1:67-80.
The Saviour and His Forerunner. As soon as Zacharias had regained his ability to speak, he was filled with the Holy Spirit and burst forth into a hymn of praise to Yahweh for His faithfulness to Israel. Zacharias prophesied both about the ministry of his son, John the Baptist, and about that of the Christ for whom John would prepare the way. This is what all the patriarchs and prophets had been waiting for.

TUESDAY, Feb. 28.   John 1:29-34.
The Lamb of God. Here we have the official testimony of Messiah's herald to the identity of His Lord. Jesus is the Lamb of God, the fulfillment not only of the Passover lamb but of all the sin offerings from the time of Aaron down to Caiaphas himself, who unknowingly prophesied of this very fact (cf. 11:49-51).

WEDNESDAY, Mar. 1.   Matt. 3:1-12.
Make way for the Lord. The image would have been unmistakable for anyone to recognize: here was Elijah, returned to herald Messiah's coming! John's message was all about separation: the repentant sinners from the "brood of vipers" represented by the Pharisees, the true, spiritual children of Abraham from those of his descendants after the flesh who remained faithless, the "trees" bearing good fruit from those bearing evil fruit, the "wheat" from the "chaff."

THURSDAY, Mar. 2.   Mark 9:2-8.
Listen to My Son. The apostle John would later write in his first epistle of this experience of witnessing the unveiled glory of God the Son (cf. I John 1:1-4). The transfiguration left Peter, James, and John "sore afraid" and speechless. Peter, ever the impulsive one before Pentecost, began to babble about building three tabernacles; as if Moses and Elijah were somehow equal with the eternal Son! Rebuking Peter's error, God the Father Himself appeared in the glory cloud of old, declaring that Jesus alone is His beloved Son; He alone is the Word of God.

FRIDAY, Mar. 3.   John 12:27-32.
A voice from heaven. On the eve of His darkest hour, the Son of God was deeply distressed at the prospect of His own impending torture and death. But deliverance was not an option; for this was the very reason for His incarnation, His birth, His life, and His ministry: to suffer and die for the sins of the whole world (cf. I John 2:2). As a sign to those gathered around Him that His prayer had been heard, the very voice of God the Father thundered from heaven: God would indeed glorify Himself through His Son.

SATURDAY, Mar. 4.   II Pet. 1:16-21.
Eyewitnesses to Christ's majesty. As John had done in his epistle (I John 1:1-4), so Peter did in his. He recounted his own testimony of the glory of the transfigured Son of God on the "holy mount." He himself had heard the very voice of God echo from the highest heaven: "This is my beloved Son, in whom I am well pleased."

SUNDAY, Mar. 5.   Mark 1:4-13.
The beloved Son. In the spirit and power of Elijah, John came baptizing those who were repentant of their sins in preparation of Messiah's arrival. But then appeared One who had nothing to repent, seeking to fulfill all righteousness by submitting to John's baptism (cf. Matt. 3:15), fully identifying with the repentant sinners He had come to save by giving His life in their place.

—*John Lody.*

SCRIPTURE LESSON TEXT

MATT. 4:1 Then was Jesus led up of the Spirit into the wilderness to be tempted of the devil.

2 And when he had fasted forty days and forty nights, he was afterward an hungred.

3 And when the tempter came to him, he said, If thou be the Son of God, command that these stones be made bread.

4 But he answered and said, It is written, Man shall not live by bread alone, but by every word that proceedeth out of the mouth of God.

5 Then the devil taketh him up into the holy city, and setteth him on a pinnacle of the temple,

6 And saith unto him, If thou be the Son of God, cast thyself down: for it is written, He shall give his angels charge concerning thee: and in *their* hands they shall bear thee up, lest at any time thou dash thy foot against a stone.

7 Jesus said unto him, It is written again, Thou shalt not tempt the Lord thy God.

8 Again, the devil taketh him up into an exceeding high mountain, and sheweth him all the kingdoms of the world, and the glory of them;

9 And saith unto him, All these things will I give thee, if thou wilt fall down and worship me.

10 Then saith Jesus unto him, Get thee hence, Satan: for it is written, Thou shalt worship the Lord thy God, and him only shalt thou serve.

11 Then the devil leaveth him, and, behold, angels came and ministered unto him.

12 Now when Jesus had heard that John was cast into prison, he departed into Galilee;

13 And leaving Nazareth, he came and dwelt in Capernaum, which is upon the sea coast, in the borders of Zabulon and Nephthalim:

14 That it might be fulfilled which was spoken by Esaias the prophet.

NOTES

Overcoming Temptation with the Word

Lesson Text: Matthew 4:1-14*a*

Related Scriptures: Luke 4:1-13; I Corinthians 10:9-13; I John 2:12-14

TIME: A.D. 26   PLACE: wilderness of Judea

GOLDEN TEXT—"But he answered and said, It is written, Man shall not live by bread alone, but by every word that proceedeth out of the mouth of God" (Matthew 4:4).

Lesson Exposition

This week's lesson is about Satan's temptation of Jesus. His temptation helped Jesus understand what it is like to be tempted, uniquely qualifying Him to be our High Priest so that He might intervene with the Father on our behalf.

God's Word states, "We have not an high priest which cannot be touched with the feeling of our infirmities; but was in all points tempted like as we are, yet without sin" (Heb. 4:15). God the Son experienced the power of temptation in the context of human weakness. This enabled Him to understand the power of temptation and effectively plead our case before God the Father.

It is important to understand the nature of Jesus' temptations. These temptations were designed by Satan to exploit Jesus in areas in which all humans are vulnerable. Satan undoubtedly thought that God's Son's appearing in human flesh would provide him the opportunity to defeat God's purposes. He would attempt to foil the plan of God in the moment of Jesus' greatest physical weakness.

THE TEMPTATION OF APPETITE—Matt. 4:1-4

Led by God's Spirit (Matt. 4:1). Jesus was sensitive to the leading of the Holy Spirit. The Spirit led Jesus to a wilderness location in Judea. The term "wilderness" does not mean wasteland; rather, it means a solitary, deserted area not inhabited by man. Only wild animals lived there (Mark 1:13). Nothing there would comfort Jesus or make life easy. In this solitary place, Jesus would meet Satan, the enemy of mankind.

Physically hungry (Matt. 4:2). No worthwhile plants grew in the Judean wilderness. Jesus therefore went without physical sustenance for forty days. He would be physically weak and hungry.

The first temptation (Matt. 4:3). It must be understood that Satan's challenge to Jesus was twofold. There was certainly the challenge to miraculously turn rock into bread and satisfy physical hunger. Jesus was hungry. There was also, however, a more subtle challenge both here and in the second temptation. Do not overlook the phrase

"If thou be the Son of God." Satan was looking for some weakness in Jesus' sense of who He was and is. Satan's greatest weapon against man is doubt. He tried to use it on the God-Man. It did not work! Jesus was certain of His identity as the Son of God.

Recognizing His dependency (Matt. 4:4). In each of the three temptations, Jesus countered Satan by using God's Word. In this instance, He quoted Deuteronomy 8:3. Even though Jesus knew He was God, He was not hesitant to express an unquestioned dependence on His Father. Jesus knew that doing the will of the Father was more important than eating any meal. Jesus said, "My meat is to do the will of him that sent me, and to finish his work" (John 4:34). Satan tries to sidetrack us from doing God's work by having us focus on physical matters. The wise Christian will not fall prey to that ploy.

Human appetites are powerful. Satan uses those appetites to lure us into sin. We are tempted when we are offered something enticing that is contrary to God's will, and we must make a choice whether we will obey God. Being certain of who we are in Christ and of our own dependence on God will help us gain victory over human appetites.

THE TEMPTATION OF AUDACITY— Matt. 4:5-7

The pinnacle site (Matt. 4:5). Satan transported Jesus to the highest point of the temple in Jerusalem. The Kidron Valley sloped down steeply from the southeast corner of Herod's temple. From the roof's edge overhanging Herod's portico to the bottom of the valley was about 450 feet. A fall from that point would have been fatal.

The promise (Matt. 4:6). Satan knows Scripture. He knew the promise of safety given in Psalm 91:11-12. He tempted Jesus with an opportunity to audaciously put God to the test. He was tempting Jesus to show off and coerce His Father into performing a miracle to save Him.

The problem (Matt. 4:7). Jesus again countered with Scripture. He quoted Deuteronomy 6:16. We are not to put God to the test. Jesus would do miracles, but He would not put His life in jeopardy just to bring about a miraculous deliverance from His Father. God would later provide His Son a miraculous deliverance from death, but this would be in His own time and His own way. We call it the resurrection!

The power of the temptation of audacity is strong in the human heart. If we could make God do what we want when we want it done, He would become our servant rather than our Master.

THE TEMPTATION OF AMBITION— Matt. 4:8-11

Satan's deal (Matt. 4:8-9). We have a crafty adversary in Satan. Recognizing his failure to get Jesus to disobey the Father's will, Satan offered a most potent temptation. He took Jesus to a mountain from which they could see all the kingdoms of the world. Surveying all that was spread before them, Satan offered everything to Jesus if Jesus would bow down and worship him.

Note that the phrase questioning Jesus' identity had been dropped by this point. Satan knew he would not be successful in getting Jesus to doubt He was God's Son.

A question arises. Were these kingdoms Satan's to offer? Is not God the Ruler of the universe? The Lord certainly is the Ruler of the universe; yet Satan rules the hearts of the ungodly. He is called "the god of this world" (II Cor. 4:4); so Satan was making a legitimate offer.

God's command (Matt. 4:10). Jesus told Satan to get away, for what we worship rules us. Jesus was not going to offer Satan the opportunity to rule Him by worshipping Satan for one second. Jesus referred to Deuteronomy 6:13 and 10:20, citing the Lord's requirement that man serve Him alone. If Jesus had capitulated to Satan, He would have violated the first commandment: "Thou shalt have no other gods before me" (Ex. 20:3).

This was a temptation of ambition. Scripture prophesied that the Messiah would sit on David's throne (cf. II Sam. 7:12-16). It was not a kingdom of worldly principalities, however. His kingdom would not be of this world (John 18:36). He would rule men's hearts (Luke 17:20-21) as well as establish an earthly kingdom (Mic. 4:1-5; Zech. 14:1-5, 9, 16).

If Jesus had been susceptible to the temptation of ambition, He would have taken Satan's offer and circumvented the plan of His Father, which was that He die for our sins. How tragic that would have been! Satan found that not even ambition would overwhelm the Son of God. Jesus' greatest ambition was to do the will of His Father (John 6:38). That did not include worshipping Satan!

Satan's defeat (Matt. 4:11). We dare not accuse Satan of being stupid. He knew he had been beaten; so he left Jesus alone. Satan's departure, however, was not permanent. He departed from Him only for a season (Luke 4:13).

THE TRUTH OF PROPHECY—
Matt. 4:12-14a

Returning to Galilee (Matt. 4:12). Immediately after His temptations, Jesus returned to where John the Baptist had been baptizing (John 1:29-43). It seems that John the Baptist was imprisoned a short time later for condemning Herod for living with his brother's wife (Matt. 14:1-5). Jesus therefore returned to Galilee. He apparently went home to Nazareth.

Fulfilling prophecy (Matt. 4:13-14a). Jesus moved from Nazareth to Capernaum after His miracle at Cana (John 2:11-12). Capernaum was on the northwest shore of the Sea of Galilee. This city would serve as His headquarters for the Galilean ministry.

Even in His travels, Jesus did the will of God and fulfilled Scripture. By going to Galilee, Jesus fulfilled a prophecy of Isaiah, given some seven hundred years before His birth (Matt. 4:14; cf. Isa. 9:1-2).

Satan's desire to test Jesus is a powerful reminder that none of us is beyond the power of temptation (cf. I Cor. 10:6-12). Whether appetite, audacity, or ambition, all of us have our weaknesses. Jesus is our example as to how to resist temptation and defeat Satan's attempts to lure us into sin.
—Terry Clark.

PRACTICAL POINTS

1. Physical weakness often opens the door to temptation (Matt. 4:1-2).
2. Satan is always eager to have us satisfy the desires of the flesh (vs. 3).
3. Scripture provides the most effective weapon against the wiles of Satan (vs. 4).
4. Satan knows Scripture and will take it out of context if that serves his purpose (vss. 5-6).
5. God does not appreciate those who twist His words and try to use them against Him (vs. 7).
6. God alone is worthy of man's worship. To offer worship to Satan is an abomination (vss. 8-10).
7. Times of temptation wax and wane. When temptations lessen, we must still be careful to follow God's leading (vss. 11-14).
—Terry Clark.

FOR DAILY MEDITATION

MONDAY, Mar. 6.   Deut. 8:1-10.

God's care in the wilderness. Verse 3 was quoted by the Lord Jesus to rebuke Satan during His temptation in the wilderness. To satisfy His intense hunger after a forty-day fast, Satan challenged Him to use His divine power to change stones into bread. But as the fulfillment of all that Israel had been intended to be, Jesus would prevail where Israel had failed. He would resist all temptations from the world, the flesh, and the devil to keep all God's commandments perfectly, and thus to secure our salvation.

TUESDAY, Mar. 7.   Ps. 95:1-11.

Worship and trust God. Psalm 95 calls for us to worship and celebrate the glory and majesty of Yahweh as the supreme Ruler over all the universe. But it also cautions us not to harden our hearts toward His Word, as Israel did when they provoked His wrath by refusing to trust Him to give them victory over the nations of Canaan. We have every reason to trust Him based on the sacrifice of His beloved Son for our salvation.

WEDNESDAY, Mar. 8.   Jas. 4:7-12.

Resist the devil. When we speak evil of fellow Christians, we set ourselves against God's grace in Christ, placing ourselves on the side of Satan, "the accuser of our brethren" (cf. Rev. 12:9-11). Satan's accusations are based on violations of God's law. The only escape is through humbling ourselves before the Lord in repentance, trusting in His grace in Christ alone.

THURSDAY, Mar. 9.   Eph. 6:10-20.

The whole armor of God. We must be careful to remember that our spiritual warfare is not against people.

Human beings, no matter how disagreeable or hateful they may behave, are not our enemies; they are merely deceived by Satan as we all once were before faith in Christ.

FRIDAY, Mar. 10.   I Cor. 10:9-13.

Stand against temptation. Paul cited the Israelites' provocation of the Lord in Exodus and Numbers as a warning to his readers. Just as the Israelites presumed on the patience and mercy of Yahweh, Christians are often tempted to presume on the mercy and grace that He has lavished on them in Christ. But the same Yahweh is faithful to provide the means for us to resist any such temptation.

SATURDAY, Mar. 11.   I Pet. 5:6-11.

Cast your cares upon Him. Peter extolled the benefits of humility as necessary to the Christian life. Since we trust that God has promised to exalt us to heaven for Christ's sake, we should be willing to embrace humility now. Knowing that God cares for us with the same love that caused Him to send Jesus to die for us, we should feel confident to leave all our worries in His hands.

SUNDAY, Mar. 12. Matt. 4:1-14*a*.

Temptation in the wilderness. Satan tempted Christ in the three most compelling areas: physical necessity, personal identity, and the will to power. The needs of the body are basic and undeniable. But Satan will always tempt us to go beyond God's provision for them to gratify ourselves in ways that God has forbidden. God has created us in His image and for His glory. But Satan will always tempt us to either exalt ourselves beyond measure or to devalue ourselves as worthless. God has made us His stewards over creation, but Satan will always tempt us to usurp the place of God.

—John Lody.

SCRIPTURE LESSON TEXT

JOHN 5:19 Then answered Jesus and said unto them, Verily, verily, I say unto you, The Son can do nothing of himself, but what he seeth the Father do: for what things soever he doeth, these also doeth the Son likewise.

20 For the Father loveth the Son, and sheweth him all things that himself doeth: and he will shew him greater works than these, that ye may marvel.

21 For as the Father raiseth up the dead, and quickeneth *them;* even so the Son quickeneth whom he will.

22 For the Father judgeth no man, but hath committed all judgment unto the Son:

23 That all *men* should honour the Son, even as they honour the Father. He that honoureth not the Son honoureth not the Father which hath sent him.

24 Verily, verily, I say unto you, He that heareth my word, and believeth on him that sent me, hath everlasting life, and shall not come into condemnation; but is passed from death unto life.

25 Verily, verily, I say unto you, The hour is coming, and now is, when the dead shall hear the voice of the Son of God: and they that hear shall live.

26 For as the Father hath life in himself; so hath he given to the Son to have life in himself;

27 And hath given him authority to execute judgment also, because he is the Son of man.

28 Marvel not at this: for the hour is coming, in the which all that are in the graves shall hear his voice,

29 And shall come forth; they that have done good, unto the resurrection of life; and they that have done evil, unto the resurrection of damnation.

NOTES

Doing the Father's Work

Lesson Text: John 5:19-29

Related Scriptures: Luke 2:41-52;
John 5:1-17; 8:25-30; 10:31-39; Philippians 2:5-11

TIME: A.D. 28   PLACE: Jerusalem

GOLDEN TEXT—"Verily, verily, I say unto you, He that heareth my word, and believeth on him that sent me, hath everlasting life, and shall not come into condemnation; but is passed from death unto life" (John 5:24).

Lesson Exposition

Our lesson this week focuses on how Jesus pleased His Father by doing the works God the Father sent Him to do. Because Jesus obeyed the Father, God was pleased with Him. Jesus shares all authority and honor with the Father. All authority and power are given to Jesus because He honored the Father. Jesus gives life with authority. He taught with authority. He healed with authority. One day, He will judge with authority. Believers should honor the Son and look forward to His coming. Unbelievers need to trust in Him.

JESUS' AUTHORITY—John 5:19-23

Authority from the Father (John 5:19-20). From His childhood, Jesus had learned submission to His earthly father. Now we see how He stays submissive to His heavenly Father. He Himself stated that He could do nothing by Himself. Everything He does is a divine extension of what His heavenly Father wants. The Son, Jesus, does everything the Heavenly Father does. This speaks to the deeply intimate relationship that they have with each other. They have such a high degree of unity that there is no possibility of disagreement.

Jesus went on to explain that the authority that He was given by the Father will lead Him to do even greater things than the healing of the lame man that He had just done (cf. vss. 1-13). The world would be astonished and surprised by the things that were yet to be done by the Son.

Works of the Father and the Son (John 5:21-22). Since this is delegated authority from the Father, we see that the Son will do whatever the Father does. He will even raise the dead to life, for nothing is impossible for either the Father or the Son. The Father has also delegated all judgment to the Son. This is truly delegated authority.

Equally shared honor (John 5:23). Jesus explained that all this is done so that the world will ultimately see how the Father loves Him and thus will honor Him. We are similarly called to honor Jesus, and if we do not, we are dishonoring the Father, who sent Jesus to us. Dishonoring Jesus is equivalent to dishonoring God, for Jesus is God

Incarnate, that is, God made visible for us.

Here we are reminded that Jesus is worthy of all honor. The Father has made this plain to the world by putting all the authority in His hands. The world is called to recognize this authority and honor Jesus too. The truth is that if we do not, one day we will recognize His authority and honor Him even though it is against our will, for Jesus is truly Lord of all. God the Heavenly Father has declared this before all men.

AUTHORITY TO GIVE LIFE—
John 5:24

In this brief verse, we find the message of the gospel in a nutshell. Jesus made a public declaration of this before His hearers.

Jesus mentioned that two things had to be done with the message that He preached. First, it had to be heard clearly. This means that people must have open ears so that the message is received with an open heart and mind. The world is always looking for a message that sustains. Jesus' message promises to be that kind of message. It is a message that promises eternal life.

The second thing that Jesus mentioned is that this message must be believed with the heart after it has been received. Jesus said that this was a message sent from God Himself. There was no other message like it in all the world, and there never will be, for it is unique in its offer of salvation for the whole world. If the message is not believed, it will fall by the wayside. It will then become a wasted message. This message dare not be wasted, for it comes at a very costly price that Jesus Himself paid.

Believing in this important message that Jesus proclaimed will have two results. First, believers will be free from the condemnation of sin. Jesus showed us the way. We are called to believe in Him and the work that He has already done for us on the cross. This is the way to be free from condemnation.

As we look at the world around us, we see people following many ways to be free. But they are definitely going the wrong way as they seek freedom, for the Scriptures declare to us that Jesus is the only way there is to true freedom from the condemnation of our sin.

Second, we are reminded here that he who believes has already passed from death to life. It is instantaneous, and we will know it when it happens. It is a time of celebration, and it comes as we believe in the One who has been sent to us from God. The Bible reminds us that even the angels rejoice and celebrate when one person on earth makes that serious commitment to believe and trust in Jesus and His message. When a person believes, he is bound for heaven, which is now his eternal home.

AUTHORITY TO JUDGE—
John 5:25-29

The One who has life (John 5:25-26). The world is looking for eternal life and freedom from the shackles of this sinful world, but people always end up disappointed when they look anywhere other than Jesus.

Jesus reminded His hearers that the day was coming when the voice of the Son of God would trumpet loudly, and even the dead would hear His voice and rise up again and live. In other words, there is life-giving power in the message that Jesus delivers. Those who listen to His words will live forever.

God the Father has life in Himself, and He has given that same life to His Son so that all who look to Him can live through that life that He offers to all. This life is eternal in nature and sets us truly free.

Jesus said that if anyone comes to

Him, He will give them water so that they will never thirst again (4:14). He offers eternal life, which cannot be found anywhere else or in any other way except through believing in Him.

We know this is true because He was sent by God and from God. Jesus said so Himself, and His life proved it. The offer still stands today, and He honors His promise to all who come to Him. He still gives life today.

The One who will sit in judgment (John 5:27). Not only does Jesus give us life, but He also has been appointed Judge over all of us. Many religions affirm their belief in a final judgment. Islam is one of them. Christianity, however, is unique in that it affirms that Jesus alone will be our final Judge, for the Father has given that authority to Him. We know who our Judge is.

Jesus said that He was given this authority because He was the Son of Man. This title implies that Jesus knows our nature because He was one of us (cf. Heb. 4:14-16) He knows the weakness of our bodies and our mindset. He suffered as we do and has walked in our shoes, so He knows what we go through.

The great division (John 5:28-29). Not only does Jesus know our weaknesses, but He also is fit to judge us for that very reason. Jesus reminded His hearers that it will not be long before the voice of the Son of Man will raise the dead. This will be the clarion call for judgment. Jesus will be on the throne, and He will be set to judge the world. The dead will hear His voice and rise again. Some will rise to eternal life and others to eternal damnation.

The Jews, however, were shocked by Jesus' claims. It seemed to them the height of arrogance for Him to assert that He had the authority to judge the whole world. Not only that, but this judgment is also to be based specifically on how people respond to the message of Jesus during their lives on earth and not merely on good works or religious practices.

This truth, of course, applies to those who are alive today, for one day we all will be judged.

Jesus said that His judgment is just, for He always does what His Father wants. He always follows the will of the Father.

As Christians, we have nothing to fear if we have acknowledged what Jesus did for us and believe His message. We are called to share this message with others who do not know Jesus so that they will not face condemnation for sin but will know eternal life in Jesus. It is given to all who will trust in Him.

—A. Koshy Muthalaly.

PRACTICAL POINTS

1. We can trust Jesus, for He received His authority from God the Father (John 5:19-20).

2. God the Father has imparted life and judgment to Jesus (vss. 21-22).

3. We are told to honor Jesus the Son if we are to please God (vs. 23).

4. We are to hear the message that Jesus came to bring us. After we hear the message, we are to believe and receive it for eternal life (vs. 24).

5. Jesus the Son alone gives life to all the world (vss. 25-26).

6. The Son has been given authority by God to judge the whole world (vs. 27).

7. Jesus will be the Judge of all mankind, and we will all have to stand before Him one day (vss. 28-29).

—A. Koshy Muthalaly.

FOR DAILY MEDITATION

MONDAY, Mar. 13.   John 5:1-17.

Made whole by the Son. Jesus looked at this man, who for thirty-eight years had struggled with his ailment, whatever it was. As the lame man waited for the angel to stir the waters, suddenly a much greater Healer had arrived right in front of him—the Creator of the universe Himself! But the petty, obsessed with their own made-up rules, desired only that this good deed would not go unpunished. Sadly, they had no understanding of how God really works.

TUESDAY, Mar. 14.   Luke 2:41-52.

In the Father's house. "Where is Jesus?" "I thought He was with your family!" "I thought He was with yours!" "No one has seen Him since we left Jerusalem!" Imagine the frantic, three-day search around the city for their lost son. They found Him in the temple, conversing with the learned men. "Oh, Jesus, why have You done this to us!" "But, Mother, you should have known I would be at My Father's house, doing My Father's business!" He answered.

WEDNESDAY, Mar. 15.
Luke 10:17-24.

Jesus praises His Father. Jesus praised His Father for the same thing Paul wrote about in I Corinthians 1:18-29. God works through the most unlikely people to confound the world. The world will never be impressed by God's power as it is manifested in His servants. The world looks for the very things that God so seldom chooses to use for His glory. The world has no time for the things that prophets and kings have longed for centuries to see and hear. The most precious gift is a person's name written in heaven.

THURSDAY, Mar. 16.
John 10:31-39.

Jesus does what His Father does. Jesus forcefully made His point; His claims were borne out by the works He does. Just because a human being claims to be God does not constitute blasphemy. After all, had the Jews not been awaiting the coming Messiah? How could they ever hope to recognize Messiah, since He Himself would claim to be God? Jesus' entire earthly life was a proof of His divine claims.

FRIDAY, Mar. 17.   John 8:25-30.

Doing the Father's will. By predicting the manner of His own death, Jesus was giving His hearers a prophecy and a sign to prove to them who He is. When they saw Him lifted up on the cross, they would have ample proof to realize who He is, since He foretold it in their very hearing. So powerful were Jesus' words that many who heard them believed on the spot!

SATURDAY, Mar. 18.
John 14:28-31.

Obeying the Father. Jesus and His disciples were just about to leave the upper room, where they had been observing the Passover, and journey to the Garden of Gethsemane. But before they went, Jesus wanted to assure them that, despite how sad they felt because He was going away, they should be joyful that He was going to His Father so that they would see the eternal reality behind the coming heartbreak and horror of His crucifixion.

SUNDAY, Mar. 19.   John 5:19-29.

The Son honors the Father. Jesus is to be honored as the Son of God. Failure to honor Christ is tantamount to dishonoring God the Father. At the resurrection, the difference between being raised to eternal life or being raised to eternal damnation is whether we honor Jesus correctly.

—John Lody.

SCRIPTURE LESSON TEXT

MATT. 26:36 Then cometh Jesus with them unto a place called Gethsemane, and saith unto the disciples, Sit ye here, while I go and pray yonder.

37 And he took with him Peter and the two sons of Zebedee, and began to be sorrowful and very heavy.

38 Then saith he unto them, My soul is exceeding sorrowful, even unto death: tarry ye here, and watch with me.

39 And he went a little further, and fell on his face, and prayed, saying, O my Father, if it be possible, let this cup pass from me: nevertheless not as I will, but as thou *wilt.*

40 And he cometh unto the disciples, and findeth them asleep, and saith unto Peter, What, could ye not watch with me one hour?

41 Watch and pray, that ye enter not into temptation: the spirit indeed *is* willing, but the flesh *is* weak.

42 He went away again the second time, and prayed, saying, O my Father, if this cup may not pass away from me, except I drink it, thy will be done.

43 And he came and found them asleep again: for their eyes were heavy.

44 And he left them, and went away again, and prayed the third time, saying the same words.

45 Then cometh he to his disciples, and saith unto them, Sleep on now, and take *your* rest: behold, the hour is at hand, and the Son of man is betrayed into the hands of sinners.

46 Rise, let us be going: behold, he is at hand that doth betray me.

47 And while he yet spake, lo, Judas, one of the twelve, came, and with him a great multitude with swords and staves, from the chief priests and elders of the people.

48 Now he that betrayed him gave them a sign, saying, Whomsoever I shall kiss, that same is he: hold him fast.

49 And forthwith he came to Jesus, and said, Hail, master; and kissed him.

50 And Jesus said unto him, Friend, wherefore art thou come? Then came they, and laid hands on Jesus, and took him.

NOTES

Submitting to the Father's Will

Lesson Text: Matthew 26:36-50

Related Scriptures: Psalm 88:1-18; Mark 14:32-42;
John 12:20-26; Hebrews 5:7-9

TIME: A.D. 30   PLACE: Mount of Olives

GOLDEN TEXT—"And he went a little further, and fell on his face, and prayed, saying, O my Father, if it be possible, let this cup pass from me: nevertheless not as I will, but as thou wilt" (Matthew 26:39).

Lesson Exposition

STRUGGLES IN GETHSEMANE— Matt. 26:36-46

"Gethsemane" means "oil press." It was on the slope of the Mount of Olives, a 2,700-foot hill overlooking the temple area from the east. Evidently, Jesus often went to this place of solitude to pray (cf. Luke 22:39).

Instructing the disciples to pray (Matt. 26:36-38). Judas had left, and Jesus took the other eleven disciples to Gethsemane. Jesus and His men had apparently come here often (John 18:1-2). He left eight of them to pray in the outer garden and took three disciples farther. It appears that Peter, James, and John were an inner circle (cf. Matt. 17:1).

"It may be significant that it is these three who have explicitly declared their readiness to share Jesus' fate (20:22; 26:35); they are now called to share with him in preparing for it, and even at this level they will fail" (France, *The Gospel According to Matthew,* Eerdmans).

These three disciples, and others, would learn to depend on God instead of their own power.

Gaining victory over the flesh (Matt. 26:39). Jesus knew what was soon to come, and He dreaded it. Not only would He face terrible physical pain, but He also would face the emotional pain of betrayal and rejection from His own creation. Even His heavenly Father would turn away while Jesus bore our sin. That was the worst. He would face spiritual pain and separation. Sorrow and anguish fell heavily upon Jesus.

Jesus could have been strengthened by the prayer support of these three close friends who had sworn their allegiance, so He instructed the three to pray and went a stone's throw away to talk alone with His Father (cf. Luke 22:40-41).

The weight of sorrow was so heavy that Jesus fell on His face. This is a submissive position. It also is a vulnerable position for one who was expecting His enemies to come soon. Jesus used His last free hours to focus on fervent prayer. James told us, "The effectual fervent prayer of a righteous man availeth much" (Jas. 5:16).

What is the "cup" (Matt. 26:39) our holy Jesus asked the Father to remove if possible? In several places, the Word mentions a cup full of God's wrath against sin (cf. Ps. 11:6; Isa. 51:17; Jer. 25:15). This is the cup the Father was handing Jesus. The awful horror of taking on the sins of the world could be surpassed only by knowing He would drink the cup of God's wrath.

Of course, the sinless Messiah did not want to accept that. His flesh recoiled from the physical and emotional pain. His deity was repulsed by the spiritual death He would suffer; yet He knew there was no other way of redeeming mankind. He had committed Himself to this mission, and now it was upon Him. Driven by love, He continued down the road to death God had chosen from the foundation of the earth (cf. I Pet. 1:18-20).

Luke told us an angel came to strengthen Jesus. He was in such agony that "his sweat was as it were great drops of blood falling down to the ground" (Luke 22:44).

Losing the battle against the flesh (Matt. 26:40-46). When Jesus returned to His friends, He found them sleeping. He said to Peter, "What, could ye not watch with me one hour?"

Do we ever forget we are in the heat of spiritual battle when we pray? Is it wise to sleep in the midst of a battle?

Jesus admonished the disciples to pray so that they would not give in to temptation during the tests they would soon endure. Before daylight, they must have wished they had heeded His warning.

Jesus left and prayed a second time. This time Jesus said, "If this cup may not pass away from me, except I drink it, thy will be done" (vs. 42). During His first prayer, Jesus yielded to the Father's will—taking the cup. This time Jesus submitted to drinking the contents. There seems to be a progression in these two prayers.

Returning a second time, Jesus found the disciples asleep again. The Word does not say He woke them. "He left them, and went away again, and prayed the third time" (vs. 44). This time He prayed the same words. Jesus won over the flesh by faith. He knew how much His Father loved Him, He knew what His mission would accomplish, and He desired the Father's will above all else.

When Jesus returned after His third prayer, He woke the disciples again. There are conflicting ideas about the phrase in Matthew 26:45, translated in the King James Version, "Sleep on now, and take your rest," because the verbs can be taken as either imperative or indicative. Some believe it was spoken sarcastically, but that does not fit with the context. J. Vernon McGee wrote that there is a space of time between this phrase and the next, "Behold, the hour is at hand" (*Thru the Bible,* Nelson). Another possibility is to "construe the verbs as indicatives and to give the sentence an interrogative form. It then becomes another expression of pained surprise." It would sound like "Are you still sleeping and taking your rest?" (Tasker, *The Gospel According to St. Matthew,* Eerdmans).

Any way we read it, all naps were ended when Jesus said, "Rise, let us be going: behold, he is at hand that doth betray me" (vs. 46). Jesus did not run away but went to face His enemies.

BETRAYAL IN GETHSEMANE— Matt. 26:47-50

Judas with the mob to arrest Jesus (Matt. 26:47-49). Judas knew Jesus would probably be at Gethsemane. "For Jesus ofttimes resorted thither with his disciples" (John 18:2). There is no record of Jesus spending a night in the walled city of Jerusalem.

"Judas then, having received a band of men and officers from the chief priests and Pharisees, cometh thither with lanterns and torches and weapons" (vs. 3). A "band" was one tenth of a legion. At that time, a Roman legion included between three thousand and six thousand men if the legion was at full strength. Several hundred armed men came to arrest Jesus. John only says they had weapons. Matthew and Mark say they came with swords and clubs (cf. Mark 14:43).

It was not unusual for a man to greet a friend with a kiss on the cheek. This, however, was not a greeting but a sign to identify Jesus for His enemies. This was the worst betrayal in history, and the Judas kiss has become infamous.

Jesus' submission to arrest (Matt. 26:50). Jesus called Judas His friend even during the betrayal. Judas showed no signs of true repentance. His heart was so hardened by then that it was too late.

It does not matter how many people came with what type of weapons. They could not have arrested Jesus unless He consented to it.

The mob was well armed for normal physical battle, but this was a spiritual warfare about which they knew nothing. Jesus could have called an innumerable number of angels to defend Him, but He yielded to mere mortals so that the prophecies about the Messiah would be fulfilled (cf. vss. 53-54).

Jesus fulfilled many Old Testament Scriptures in His lifetime. Some that apply to this lesson include: "I was not rebellious, neither turned away back" (Isa. 50:5) and "He is despised and rejected of men; a man of sorrows, and acquainted with grief" (53:3).

Because Jesus had drawn strength from His Father during Their prayer time, He was able to face His attackers. According to John's testimony, Jesus asked the mob, "Whom seek ye?" (John 18:4).

"They answered him, Jesus of Nazareth. Jesus saith unto them, I am *he*" (vs. 5). Notice that "he" is in italics. That means it was added for clarity. Literally, Jesus said, "I am."

When God had talked to Moses from the burning bush, He identified Himself as "I AM" (Ex. 3:14).

How did the mob who came to arrest Jesus react to His statement? "They went backward, and fell to the ground" (John 18:6).

This did not stop the mob from arresting Jesus, but they had an opportunity to see Him as more than a mere man. Why did they not recognize the deity of Jesus? Why did they not repent and beg His forgiveness? Why do people still fail to do this?

—Arlene Knickerbocker.

PRACTICAL POINTS

1. It is important to support others as they endure difficult trials (Matt. 26:36-38).
2. Let us grow in grace and stay in prayer until we desire God's will above all else (vs. 39).
3. Prayer can prepare us for temptations and trials that may come upon us (vss. 40-41).
4. Sometimes it takes more than one session of prayer to align our will with God's and draw strength from Him (vss. 42-44).
5. Christians can face trials and temptations with confidence because we know God loves us and will accomplish His purpose (Matt. 26:45-49; cf. Rom. 8:28).
6. We must yield completely to our Father's will no matter what the cost here on earth. Let us keep our eyes on Jesus and our heavenly hope (Matt. 26:50).

—Arlene Knickerbocker.

FOR DAILY MEDITATION

MONDAY, Mar. 20.   Ps. 42:1-11.

Placing hope in God. This psalm is aptly associated with Christ's agony in the Garden of Gethsemane. Like Christ, the psalmist longs to feel God's nearness during a time of great inner conflict and turmoil. His adversaries seek to bring doubt and despair into his heart by pointing at his circumstances and asking, "Where is your God now?" But also, like Christ, the psalmist's trust in God is steadfast and unfailing. He reminds himself to hope in the Lord as his only salvation.

TUESDAY, Mar. 21.   John 12:20-26.

Jesus' hour has come. Jesus responds to being told that some Gentiles are seeking Him to announce that His hour had arrived. It was His time to be planted like a seed so that salvation would abound not only to the Jews but also to Gentiles throughout the world. Likewise, we who follow Him as Lord and Saviour must disdain our former lives with their fleshly desires.

**WEDNESDAY, Mar. 22.
John 16:29-33.**

Peace from trusting Jesus. The disciples declared that now they clearly understood that Jesus is really from God. They thought they had reached the summit of their discipleship. But then Jesus cast uncertainty on their assertions, saying, "So, now you really believe in Me? Well, let Me tell you something. Soon you will all desert Me and scatter to your own hidey-holes. But I will not be alone because the Father is always with Me. I know it sounds bad, but take courage; through everything that happens to Me, I will be victorious over the world!"

THURSDAY, Mar. 23.   John 17:1-5.

Jesus' work complete. Knowing that His death was imminent, Jesus began His great prayer of intercession for all His disciples—present and future. His first appeal was that God would be glorified through Him. Although His suffering and death were still ahead, He considered them an accomplished fact.

FRIDAY, Mar. 24.   John 6:37-40.

The will of Him who sent Me. It is not Jesus' job to choose who will come to Him for salvation, but the Father's. The Father has already given Him the full number of those who will trust in Him, and it is His job accept them, never lose any, and make sure they make it to the resurrection. Every last one of those who truly trusts in Him will make it; that is Jesus' job!

SATURDAY, Mar. 25.   Ps. 88:1-13.

Cry out to the Lord. Like Jesus, this psalmist plead with the Lord to hear his cries. He confessed that his soul was troubled to the point of death. Jesus, however, felt the full wrath of God that was justly intended for those for whom He died, even to the point where He was forsaken by God. But God heard His cry and abundantly answered His prayers, raising Him from the dead and exalting Him to the highest glory!

SUNDAY, Mar. 26.   Matt. 26:36-50.

Agony in the garden. Jesus came to Gethsemane to pray to His Father, being "exceeding sorrowful, even unto death." But His disciples seem to have shared none of His emotional turmoil; they kept falling asleep while they should have been watching and praying along with Him. Great agony of soul is often comforted by others sharing the burden, but Jesus bore the full weight of His agony alone.

—John Lody.

SCRIPTURE LESSON TEXT

MATT. 27:38 Then were there two thieves crucified with him, one on the right hand, and another on the left.

39 And they that passed by reviled him, wagging their heads,

40 And saying, Thou that destroyest the temple, and buildest *it* in three days, save thyself. If thou be the Son of God, come down from the cross.

41 Likewise also the chief priests mocking *him,* with the scribes and elders, said,

42 He saved others; himself he cannot save. If he be the King of Israel, let him now come down from the cross, and we will believe him.

43 He trusted in God; let him deliver him now, if he will have him: for he said, I am the Son of God.

44 The thieves also, which were crucified with him, cast the same in his teeth.

45 Now from the sixth hour there was darkness over all the land unto the ninth hour.

46 And about the ninth hour Jesus cried with a loud voice, saying, Eli, Eli, lama sabachthani? that is to say, My God, my God, why hast thou forsaken me?

47 Some of them that stood there, when they heard *that,* said, This *man* calleth for Elias.

48 And straightway one of them ran, and took a spunge, and filled *it* with vinegar, and put *it* on a reed, and gave him to drink.

49 The rest said, Let be, let us see whether Elias will come to save him.

50 Jesus, when he had cried again with a loud voice, yielded up the ghost.

51 And, behold, the veil of the temple was rent in twain from the top to the bottom; and the earth did quake, and the rocks rent;

52 And the graves were opened; and many bodies of the saints which slept arose,

53 And came out of the graves after his resurrection, and went into the holy city, and appeared unto many.

54 Now when the centurion, and they that were with him, watching Jesus, saw the earthquake, and those things that were done, they feared greatly, saying, Truly this was the Son of God.

NOTES

Crucified for Sinners

Lesson Text: Matthew 27:38-54

Related Scriptures: Psalm 22:1-18; Isaiah 53:3-12; Luke 23:32-47

TIME: A.D. 30   PLACE: Golgotha

GOLDEN TEXT—"We have seen and do testify that the Father sent the Son to be the Saviour of the world" (I John 4:14).

Lesson Exposition

This unit of study has focused on Jesus pleasing His Father by His sacrifice. The central event of His obedience to the Father's plan, His crucifixion, is the topic of this week's lesson.

This lesson discusses the climax and focal point of all history. All that went before was preparatory, and everything since flows from it. We must never let familiarity with the events dull our awareness of what happened that day. Our response to it is the difference between life and death, heaven and hell, for all people and for each of us personally.

THE TAUNTING—Matt. 27:38-44

Placed between thieves (Matt. 27:38). The Romans were experts in bringing humiliation. Although Jesus had not been convicted of a crime, He was crucified between two thieves—common criminals. This was one last expression of scorn from the Roman soldiers against Jesus, the One called Saviour. Being crucified between two vile criminals would suggest that He was considered the most notorious of the three.

The Old Testament is filled with prophecies of what took place that day. For example, Isaiah 53:12 says, "He was numbered with the transgressors; and he bare the sin of many, and made intercession for the transgressors." He was considered one of the criminals of the day. The holy and sinless Son of God was executed between two criminals and treated like the worst of them.

Reviled by common people (Matt. 27:39-40). Jesus was crucified in a very public place, just outside the city gates of Jerusalem. The Romans crucified there so that a majority of people would recognize the serious consequences of rebellion. People going in and out of the city would see those crucified, and the thought of such a death would restrain people from rebellion.

Some traveling by the crucifixion scene insulted Jesus. They apparently had heard Jesus' words (John 2:19), but they did not understand their meaning (Matt. 27:40). They therefore mocked Jesus' words. The King of the universe permitted the rabble of Israel to revile Him. He was on that cross to die for those who mocked Him. They did not yet know it, but He was dying for them (cf. Rom. 5:8).

Mocked by Israel's leaders (Matt. 27:41-43). The religious leaders of Israel taunted Jesus. They gave clear evidence of their disbelief in Him. It was not that they lacked evidence of His divine nature. His miracles had revealed that His works were of God. They realized He had saved others, yet they were unwilling to recognize Him as the Messiah.

The leaders accused Jesus of blasphemy (cf. vs. 43). Of all the people in Israel, these men should have recognized Jesus as the Messiah. Instead, they called Him a blasphemer!

Because they were experts in Old Testament studies, the religious leaders should have recognized Christ for He is. Blinded by their own pride and jealousy, they took pleasure in mocking Him. Once more, they arrogantly demanded a sign to convince them, even though He had already shown so many.

Mocked by the condemned (Matt. 27:44). Even in their suffering, the two thieves crucified with Jesus could not resist joining in with those who reviled Jesus. We know from Luke 23:39-43 that one of the two thieves later repented and acknowledged that Jesus was not guilty of a crime but was Israel's Messiah.

The official reason Jesus was executed was because He claimed to be the Son of God and the King of Israel. Those claims could have been true, or they were blasphemy against God and treason against Rome. It was those claims that all the mockers threw at Him, daring Him to prove who He said He was by freeing Himself from the cross.

What eternal loss it would have been for us had Jesus taken the dare! Jesus could have saved Himself, but He would not. The nails did not hold Him to the cross; His love and determination to purchase our salvation held Him there.

Those who were present saw only a condemned man who they could mock and scorn. Again, Old Testament prophecy was fulfilled: "He is despised and rejected of men; . . . he was despised, and we esteemed him not" (Isa. 53:3).

THE ANGUISH—Matt. 27:45-50

Being forsaken (Matt. 27:45-46). Between noon and three o'clock, darkness fell upon the earth. God was giving evidence of the desperate period earth was experiencing. Earth's Creator was becoming man's Redeemer. The Giver of life was dying so that we might live.

As if the pain of crucifixion were not enough, as Jesus was dying, He was bearing "our sins in his own body" (I Pet. 2:24; cf. Isa. 53:11). During that time, God the Father forsook Him, for our sins broke His fellowship with the Father.

Isaiah foresaw this also. He said He was "smitten of God" and that "it please the Lord to bruise him" (Isa. 53:4, 10). The gift of eternal life was only made possible by Jesus becoming sin. God is holy, and He could no longer look at Jesus. He suffered the horrible separation from the Father.

The heartache Jesus experienced was related in Aramaic (Matt. 27:46). Jesus quoted Psalm 22:1 as He hung on the cross, bearing the sins of all who would receive Him as Lord and Saviour. At the time He was suffering the penalty for our sins, He was forsaken by the Father.

Being misunderstood (Matt. 27:47-49). When Jesus called on God, some thought He was calling for Elijah to come deliver Him. It was evidently difficult for Jesus to speak (cf. John 19:28), so someone offered Him vinegar to quench His thirst. Others waited to see whether Elijah would come deliver Him.

Being true (Matt. 27:50). The Creator of life died! Jesus had fulfilled His mission (Mark 10:45). The Gospel of Matthew does not have the words Jesus shouted at the end of His ordeal. We can learn from John 19:30 that He exclaimed, "It is finished." Some might ask, "What was finished?" His suffering was over, but more than that, the mission for which He had come was complete. He had paid the full penalty for mankind's sins.

Luke 23:46 tells us that Jesus also said, "Father, into thy hands I commend my spirit." Those words show us that Jesus did not die of His wounds. Death had no power over the perfect Son of God. He voluntarily "gave up the ghost," meaning that He dismissed His spirit from His body.

THE TESTIMONY—Matt. 27:51-54

In the temple (Matt. 27:51). When Jesus died, an amazing thing happened in the temple. The curtain through which the high priest passed into the Holy of Holies only one day a year was torn from top to bottom, indicating that through Jesus people have access into God's presence (Heb. 10:19-22). An earthquake accompanied this monumental event.

Throughout Jerusalem (Matt. 27:52-54). Verses 52 and 53 are parenthetical. Historically, the people who were resurrected from the tombs appeared in Jerusalem after Jesus arose from the dead. The resurrection appearances give evidence of the fact that Jesus is the Saviour and Messiah. His death provided complete remission from sins for all believers (Rom. 3:25-26). Their resurrection appearances also reveal the truth in Luke 16:30-31 that even if some resurrected saints appeared, unbelief would continue.

On the day of Jesus' crucifixion, the Roman centurion gave testimony that the events he saw revealed that Jesus is indeed the Son of God (Matt. 27:54). Those who supposedly knew the Scriptures refused to see the truth. Pagan Romans recognized the truth. Perhaps they were the first converts from the Gentiles. The Gospels do not indicate that they became followers of Jesus, but it is possible some did.

We cannot be neutral about Jesus and His work on the cross. Every one of us stands with one group or the other. Either we refuse to recognize Christ and His claim on us, or we acknowledge Him as the Son of God, who has paid the full penalty for our sins.

—Terry Clark.

PRACTICAL POINTS

1. We should not be surprised to find Jesus in the midst of sinners (Matt. 27:38).
2. Those who do not understand Jesus' mission find it easy to revile and persecute Him (vss. 39-44).
3. In the soul's dark night, it may seem that God has forsaken us (vss. 45-46).
4. Misunderstanding what God has said has often caused people to act inappropriately and foolishly (vss. 47-49).
5. Jesus' death on the cross opened the way for man to come into the presence of God (vss. 50-52).
6. God is life. Even as His own Son died, He brought to life many people who had been dead. He has vanquished the power of death (vss. 53-54).

—Terry Clark.

FOR DAILY MEDITATION

MONDAY, Mar. 27.   Luke 23:13-31.

Jesus sentenced to die. Twice Pilate offered to release Jesus, since he could find Him guilty of no crime worthy of death. But each time the people refused, crying out for Jesus to be crucified. Finally acquiescing to their frenzied demands, Pilate had Jesus led away to be crucified. Jesus then prophesied to those gathered around, weeping for Him. He told them not to weep for Him because a greater calamity was coming upon Jerusalem. Jesus' words would be fulfilled by the events of the horrific siege and destruction of Jerusalem in A.D. 70.

TUESDAY, Mar. 28.   Ps. 22:1-18.

Christ's death foretold. The opening words of this psalm would be echoed in Jesus' cry from the cross in Aramaic, "Eli, Eli, lama sabachthani," found in Matthew 27:46. The amazing parallels between the details of Psalm 22 and Jesus' suffering during His crucifixion are too numerous and precise to be considered coincidence by even the most hardened skeptic, especially since death by crucifixion would have been completely unknown in David's time.

WEDNESDAY, Mar. 29.
John 19:16-24.

Golgotha. Pilate's resentment toward the Jewish leaders for insisting on the crucifixion of an innocent man for their own selfish ends may seem an unlikely source for a prophetic pronouncement, but we should not be too surprised, knowing that our God uses all things that come to pass to accomplish His will (cf. Eph. 1:11). Pilate's inscription above Jesus' cross unintentionally proclaimed the truth that Jesus is, in fact, the King of the Jews.

THURSDAY, Mar. 30.   Isa. 53:3-12.

The Suffering Saviour. How can the human mind comprehend the great majesty and complexity of Christ's atonement (cf. Rom. 11:33)? It is the precise focal point of God's entire redemptive plan for history—the exact intersection of humanity's most heinous sin against God and God's greatest act of love and mercy toward humanity. God's great love for sinners caused Him to sacrifice the Son He so dearly loved.

FRIDAY, Mar. 31. Luke 23:32-43.

The faith of the thief. All the world is guilty before the holy God (cf. Rom. 3:19). Thus, the two criminals can be taken as representative of the two responses to Christ among all the sinners of the world. Some hate and revile Christ, scoffing at His suffering and His offer of salvation. Others, aware of their deadly guilt before God and their need for a Saviour, rebuke these scoffers and clearly see their own guilt in the light of Christ's perfect sinlessness.

SATURDAY, Apr. 1.   John 19:28-30.

It is finished. As if the agony of crucifixion was not extreme enough, the only respite the Romans offered to its victims was a sip of sour, bitter vinegar. But this also was a fulfillment of the Scriptures (cf. Ps. 69:21). Having thus perfectly fulfilled the Father's will for Him, Jesus knew that He had made full payment for the sins of the world.

SUNDAY, Apr. 2.   Matt. 27:38-54.

Forsaken by God? Verses 39 and 43 echo Psalm 22:7-8. The image is of merciless mockery from those witnessing Jesus' mortal agony. Just imagine how their scoffing suddenly changed to fear when the earth under them began to shake violently as a sign of God the Father's indignation at their presumptuously heinous blasphemy!
—*John Lody.*

SCRIPTURE LESSON TEXT

JOHN 20:1 The first *day* of the week cometh Mary Magdalene early, when it was yet dark, unto the sepulchre, and seeth the stone taken away from the sepulchre.

2 Then she runneth, and cometh to Simon Peter, and to the other disciple, whom Jesus loved, and saith unto them, They have taken away the Lord out of the sepulchre, and we know not where they have laid him.

3 Peter therefore went forth, and that other disciple, and came to the sepulchre.

4 So they ran both together: and the other disciple did outrun Peter, and came first to the sepulchre.

5 And he stooping down, *and looking in,* saw the linen clothes lying; yet went he not in.

6 Then cometh Simon Peter following him, and went into the sepulchre, and seeth the linen clothes lie,

7 And the napkin, that was about his head, not lying with the linen clothes, but wrapped together in a place by itself.

8 Then went in also that other disciple, which came first to the sepulchre, and he saw, and believed.

9 For as yet they knew not the scripture, that he must rise again from the dead.

10 Then the disciples went away again unto their own home.

19 Then the same day at evening, being the first *day* of the week, when the doors were shut where the disciples were assembled for fear of the Jews, came Jesus and stood in the midst, and saith unto them, Peace *be* unto you.

20 And when he had so said, he shewed unto them *his* hands and his side. Then were the disciples glad, when they saw the Lord.

NOTES

Risen from the Dead!

(Easter)

Lesson Text: John 20:1-10, 19-20

Related Scriptures: Psalm 16:1-11; Luke 24:1-12;
I Corinthians 15:12-19; Ephesians 1:15-23

TIME: A.D. 30   PLACES: near Jerusalem; Jerusalem

GOLDEN TEXT—"Then the same day at evening, being the first day of the week, when the doors were shut where the disciples were assembled for fear of the Jews, came Jesus and stood in the midst, and saith unto them, Peace be unto you" (John 20:19).

Lesson Exposition

The purpose of the incarnation of Jesus Christ, the eternal Word of God, was to accomplish God's plan of redemption. To do this, it was necessary for Christ to be crucified and then to rise from the grave. His resurrection demanded a tomb emptied only by that event. His resurrection also demanded that it was He who stood in the midst of His disciples when He suddenly appeared to them.

DISCOVERY OF THE EMPTY TOMB—John 20:1-2

The first visitors (John 20:1). It was the first day of the week following Christ's crucifixion and burial. Mary Magdalene along with some other women went to the tomb to anoint the body of Jesus (Mark 16:1). She may have been the first to arrive at the tomb, so John refers just to her. Mary was devoted to Christ. He had delivered her from a terrible bondage by casting seven demons out of her (Luke 8:2).

The women came to the tomb early on Sunday morning when the day was just beginning to dawn (Mark 16:2). They were concerned about gaining entrance to the tomb, for a stone had been rolled over the doorway (vs. 3). Jesus was buried in a new rock tomb that was closed with a large stone (Matt. 27:58-60) and then sealed by Pilate's command (vss. 65-66).

To the amazement of these first visitors, the stone had been taken away from the entrance. It had been removed to permit people to discover that the tomb was empty, not to let Jesus out. Jesus' resurrection body allowed Him to leave without the necessity of an open door, just as He was able to appear suddenly to His disciples in a closed room (John 20:19, 26).

The startling report (John 20:2). Mary Magdalene immediately ran to Peter and to John in great distress over the discovery. The disciple "whom Jesus loved" (cf. 13:23-24; 19:25-27), who is also the author of this Gospel (21:24), was the apostle John. Mary and the other women were disturbed, for they assumed that grave robbers had opened the tomb and then taken Jesus' body to some undisclosed location. The thought that Jesus had risen from the dead evidently had not entered their minds. Upon hearing of the empty tomb, the Jewish leaders made up the story that the disciples had secretly stolen Jesus' body during the night (Matt. 28:11-15).

INVESTIGATION BY THE DISCIPLES—John 20:3-10

The race to the tomb (John 20:3-4). When Peter and John heard Mary Magdalene's report, they ran to the tomb. They no doubt were surprised and perplexed by Mary's story, which prompted their footrace. John won the race, arriving at the tomb ahead of Peter.

John viewed the empty tomb (John 20:5). John had to stoop down to look into the tomb because of its low opening, but for some reason he did not enter the tomb. He may have feared that he would be ceremonially defiled by touching an object connected with death.

There apparently was enough daylight by this time for John to see the linen clothing lying inside the tomb. This was evidence that no one had simply removed the body. It also meant that grave robbers had not stolen the body, for they would not have taken the time to unwrap the burial clothes from the corpse.

Joseph of Arimathea and Nicodemus saw to the burial of Jesus' body (John 19:38-40). The linen clothes were strips of linen with which the body of the deceased was wrapped (11:44). Spices were spread along the linen strips before they were wound around the body. Spices were sometimes spread directly on the body to overcome the stench of putrefaction.

Peter entered the empty tomb (John 20:6-7). Peter entered the tomb upon arrival. He also saw the graveclothes lying there without the body of Jesus. Jesus' body had passed through the linen graveclothes when He rose from the dead. Peter also saw the burial cloth folded up and lying apart from the burial clothes. This cloth was wrapped around the head to keep the jaws closed in death. Jesus had removed and folded it up because He no longer needed it.

The disciples' conclusion (John 20:8-10). John then followed Peter into the tomb. Whatever reason he had for hesitating to enter the tomb was gone. He saw the same things that Peter observed. But John perceived what the empty tomb with the burial clothes still there meant, and he believed. He saw and believed that Jesus had risen from the dead.

The two disciples did not grasp at that moment in time the teachings of Scripture that it was necessary for Christ to rise from the dead. Such Old Testament Scriptures as Psalm 16:10 and Isaiah 53:10 spoke to the necessity of Christ's resurrection. John believed that Jesus rose from the dead on seeing the evidence of the empty tomb, rather than believing the Scriptures (John 20:8-9). He came to grips with certain facts without initially relating them to the Scriptures.

Other disciples had a similar experience as Peter and John. They failed to comprehend the scriptural teaching that both Christ's death and His resurrection were necessary to God's plan of redemption (Luke 24:24-27). Ironically, the chief priests knew about Christ's foretelling of His resurrection (Matt. 27:62-66). While they did not believe in His claim, they took serious measures to prevent the fabrication of any story that He had risen from the grave. They had sought Roman soldiers from Pilate to guard the grave of Jesus.

As the author of this Gospel, John's account of his investigation of the empty tomb of Jesus and his faith response was a personal testimony on his part (John 20:8). He eventually integrated the evidence of the empty tomb with the scriptural statements on the necessity of Christ's resurrection (vs. 9). This no doubt occurred soon after his investigation.

Weeks later, Peter preached on the necessity of Christ's resurrection to the Jews who gathered in Jerusalem to celebrate the Day of Pentecost (Acts 2:14, 22-24).

Peter and John returned to their own homes after having inspected the empty tomb of Jesus.

APPEARANCE OF JESUS TO THE DISCIPLES—John 20:19-20

The sudden appearance of Jesus (John 20:19). On the evening of the day of the discovery of the empty tomb, the disciples met together. The doors of the room were bolted shut. They feared for their very lives (9:22; 19:38). Because of that fear, they met secretly. Those who had identified with Jesus faced possible persecution and even death by the Jewish leadership.

Jesus suddenly came and stood in their midst. He was unimpeded by locked doors, for His resurrection body was not subject to special limits. He was raised with a "spiritual body" (I Cor. 15:44), which is a body empowered by the Spirit. Christ is the firstfruits of the resurrection so that believers will be raised with spiritual bodies as well (vs. 23).

His greeting of "Peace" (John 20:19) was more than a typical greeting. It had the deeper meaning of inner peace, which they could have because of His victory over death and the grave (14:27).

The evidence of Jesus' identity (John 20:20). This was not an apparition but Jesus Himself. He showed them His hands and His side, for His resurrection body had the scars and wounds that identified Him. Jesus had a body of flesh and bones (Luke 24:39). He later ate with His disciples (vss. 40-43). There was continuity between the resurrection body of Christ and His body prior to His death and burial.

Jesus gave the disciples unmistakable proof that it was He and that He had conquered the grave. His scars and wounds bore witness to His suffering for their sin and that of the world. The disciples could not help having their fright changed to joy. They saw their Lord standing before them in their midst.

—*Jack Riggs.*

PRACTICAL POINTS

1. Unexpected events can blind us to what God is doing (John 20:1).
2. We can draw wrong conclusions about what God is doing if our minds are not fixed on His promises (vs. 2).
3. Our devotion to Christ should prompt us to make haste to discover the truth (vss. 3-4).
4. Jesus' resurrection had all the evidence of a historical event (vss. 5-7).
5. The object of our faith is the truth that corresponds to reality (vs. 8).
6. We can easily overlook obvious teachings in God's Word if we are not diligent (vss. 9-10).
7. We have inner peace with God only because Jesus died and rose from the dead (vss. 19-20).

—*Jack Riggs.*

FOR DAILY MEDITATION

MONDAY, Apr. 3.   Mark 16:1-11.

The stone rolled away. The women came to Jesus' tomb on the morning of the third day fully expecting to find His dead body. To their great amazement, they found the huge stone that secured the tomb's entrance already rolled away! Inside the tomb, they found only a heavenly messenger who informed them of Jesus' resurrection; but when they brought the news to His disciples, they still did not believe it! The stone of unbelief was more obstinate than the one that blocked Jesus' tomb!

TUESDAY, Apr. 4.   I Cor. 15:12-19.

No hope without resurrection. Although Christianity has abundant blessings for this present life and for the betterment of society, without the hope of the resurrection and eternal life, we are little more than just another miserable cult of deluded religious fanatics. What makes the difference is Christ's resurrection! Because He really did rise from the dead, we know that He will also really raise us from the dead.

WEDNESDAY, Apr. 5.   Eph. 1:15-23.

God's mighty power. Of all God's miracles, the resurrection of Jesus is preeminent. It alone is the consummation and vindication of God's redemptive plan for the universe. It is God's stamp of full approval on Jesus' once-for-all-time sin offering. Through it, Christ has overcome the world and made all things new for our sakes.

THURSDAY, Apr. 6.   Luke 24:1-12.

He is risen! Jesus had told them more than once. Now the women proclaimed that Jesus had risen. But the apostles still chalked it all up to "idle tales" and hysteria. Had they also so flippantly discounted Christ's own testimony about His resurrection? How right Jesus was when He said of them, "O fools, and slow of heart to believe all that the prophets have spoken" (vs. 25)!

FRIDAY, Apr. 7.   Matt. 12:38-42.

The sign of Jonah. Jesus instantly saw through the disingenuous fawning of the Pharisees as they condescended to call Him "Master." His response cut through all their pretense like a razor. Addressing them as "an evil and adulterous generation," He proceeded to tell them that the only sign they would be given was the one none of them would believe—His resurrection.

SATURDAY, Apr. 8.   Ps. 16:1-11.

Not abandoned to the grave. Peter quoted this psalm in his sermon on Pentecost (cf. Acts 2:25-33) as proof that David had prophesied about Christ's resurrection. For, since David himself did indeed die and decompose as every other mere human, he must have been looking forward to his greater Son, the Messiah.

SUNDAY, Apr. 9.   John 20:1-10, 19-20.

An empty tomb. Mark tells us that when the women reported Christ's resurrection to the apostles, they did not believe it (cf. 16:11). Luke tells us that, although Peter himself went to the tomb and looked inside, he merely wondered what had happened (cf. 24:12). John seems to have been the exception among the apostles, since he tells us here that when he saw that the tomb was empty, he believed. The natural human reaction to the assertion that Christ has risen from the dead is skepticism. True faith in the resurrection is a work of God's grace, brought about in His perfect timing.

—John Lody.

SCRIPTURE LESSON TEXT

LUKE 24:36 And as they thus spake, Jesus himself stood in the midst of them, and saith unto them, Peace *be* unto you.

37 But they were terrified and affrighted, and supposed that they had seen a spirit.

38 And he said unto them, Why are ye troubled? and why do thoughts arise in your hearts?

39 Behold my hands and my feet, that it is I myself: handle me, and see; for a spirit hath not flesh and bones, as ye see me have.

40 And when he had thus spoken, he shewed them *his* hands and *his* feet.

41 And while they yet believed not for joy, and wondered, he said unto them, Have ye here any meat?

42 And they gave him a piece of a broiled fish, and of an honeycomb.

43 And he took *it,* and did eat before them.

44 And he said unto them, These *are* the words which I spake unto you, while I was yet with you, that all things must be fulfilled, which were written in the law of Moses, and *in* the prophets, and *in* the psalms, concerning me.

45 Then opened he their understanding, that they might understand the scriptures,

46 And said unto them, Thus it is written, and thus it behoved Christ to suffer, and to rise from the dead the third day:

47 And that repentance and remission of sins should be preached in his name among all nations, beginning at Jerusalem.

48 And ye are witnesses of these things.

49 And, behold, I send the promise of my Father upon you: but tarry ye in the city of Jerusalem, until ye be endued with power from on high.

50 And he led them out as far as to Bethany, and he lifted up his hands, and blessed them.

51 And it came to pass, while he blessed them, he was parted from them, and carried up into heaven.

52 And they worshipped him, and returned to Jerusalem with great joy:

53 And were continually in the temple, praising and blessing God. Amen.

NOTES

Proofs of the Resurrection

Lesson Text: Luke 24:36-53

Related Scriptures: Acts 1:1-4; I Corinthians 15:3-8; I John 1:1-4

TIME: A.D. 30   PLACE: Jerusalem

GOLDEN TEXT—"These are the words which I spake unto you, while I was yet with you, that all things must be fulfilled, which were written in the law of Moses, and in the prophets, and in the psalms, concerning me" (Luke 24:44).

Lesson Exposition

The disciples were not easily convinced that their Master had been raised from the dead. Even as reports came from various sources on that Sunday describing His appearances, Jesus' followers were filled more with confusion, doubt, and fear than with the faith that later characterized them.

The risen Lord Jesus very patiently convinced them of His physical resurrection and allayed their fears. But this was just the first step. They needed to know the truth of His resurrection and what Scripture taught about it so that they would be prepared for the ministry they would have in the near future. And while Jesus would leave them again physically, He would also empower them for that ministry.

THE APPEARANCE OF CHRIST— Luke 24:36-43

Allaying the disciples' fears (Luke 24:36-38). "As they thus spake" indicates that the setting here is still the day of Jesus' resurrection. It was now evening, and various people had re-ported seeing the risen Jesus, including Peter (Simon), the two disciples who had returned from Emmaus, and several women.

Thomas was not present (John 20:19-24), but the other ten remaining disciples were there, along with some others. As they discussed all that had happened that day, "Jesus himself stood in the midst of them" (Luke 24:36). His appearance was sudden and supernatural, for the doors to the room were locked (John 20:19).

Jesus' first words to them were "Peace be unto you" (Luke 24:36). While this was a typical Jewish greeting, it took on added meaning here, for the disciples "were terrified and affrighted" (vs. 37), thinking they were seeing a spirit.

Jesus further asked why they were troubled with doubts (vs. 38). While many thoughts were going through their minds, it seems their chief concern was the nature of the One who stood before them. Were they seeing an apparition or one who possessed a physical body?

Giving evidence of the resurrection (Luke 24:39-43). Jesus promptly addressed this concern. He pointed to the wounds in His hands and feet and urged the disciples to touch His body. It was indeed real.

Still, the disciples "believed not for joy" (vs. 41). Intellectually, the proof was clear; but psychologically, they were hesitant to believe, thinking, as we say, it was too good to be true. They did not want to embrace a hope that could yet be shattered. Jesus then gave further evidence of His physical resurrection by eating in their presence the fish and honeycomb the disciples had with them. Clearly, Jesus was not a disembodied spirit, for only one with a physical body can eat.

The bodily resurrection of Jesus is central to our Christian faith (cf. I Cor. 15). It is the answer to any doubts that might arise in our minds. If Christ is truly risen—and He is—our hope is sure, and our faith is true. Surely that is why Jesus was so careful to give such clear evidence of His resurrection.

THE TEACHING OF CHRIST—
Luke 24:44-48

Reminders of Scripture (Luke 24:44-45). Jesus then began to teach His disciples things they needed to know. First, He reminded them of what He had previously taught them. This previous teaching was what the Old Testament said about Him, the Christ. "The law of Moses," "the prophets," and "the psalms" represent the Jews' threefold division of the Old Testament. Thus, Jesus was saying the teaching of the entire Old Testament pointed to Him and had to be fulfilled.

As He had for the disciples on the road to Emmaus, Jesus now "opened . . . their understanding" (vs. 45). Through His teaching and interpretation, the disciples now clearly saw the truth.

Requirements of Scripture (Luke 24:46-48). Specifically, the Old Testament foretold, even as Jesus Himself had, that He would suffer and die and be raised on the third day. Because God's Word proclaimed it, it had to happen this way. Jesus' presence with them now was proof that the teaching of Scripture is indeed trustworthy.

"Jesus went beyond showing how prophecy was fulfilled in his passion and resurrection. It was also fulfilled in the preaching of *repentance and forgiveness of sins*" (Morris, *Luke,* InterVarsity). Jesus may have had any number of Old Testament passages in mind (cf. Isa. 42:6; 60:3), but it was clear that God's plan required that the gospel message "be preached . . . among all nations, beginning at Jerusalem" (Luke 24:47; cf. Acts 1:8).

In short, the gospel calls on people to repent, or turn from their sin, placing their faith in Christ. This brings remission, or forgiveness, of sins (Luke 24:47). In saying the disciples were "witnesses of these things" (vs. 48), Jesus was looking ahead. They had been witnesses to His life, teaching, death, and resurrection; now they would be witnesses of who would testify to these truths and proclaim the gospel of salvation to Jews and Gentiles alike.

THE PROMISE OF GOD—
Luke 24:49

Jesus not only called His followers to be continuing witnesses to the world; He also promised them the power to carry out that calling. This refers to the Father's promise of the indwelling and empowering Holy Spirit (cf. Joel 2:28-29; John 14:16, 26).

It is comforting to know that regardless of the limitations we might have—physical, financial, intellectual, and otherwise—we who know Christ have been given the power to minister effectively for Him in our various locations and circumstances.

THE ASCENSION OF CHRIST—
Luke 24:50-53

Jesus' departure (Luke 24:50-51). While the narrative continues seamlessly here, the events described in verses 50-53 actually occurred forty days later, as Luke himself makes clear from his narrative in Acts 1:3-12. After more than a month of periodically appearing to His followers and teaching them further about the "kingdom of God," He led them out to Bethany on the Mount of Olives (Luke 24:50). There He "blessed them" and then was "carried up into heaven" (vs. 51).

"Jesus' action in . . . blessing the disciples (v. 51) was priestly. . . . [Luke] places Jesus clearly within the spiritual setting of the priesthood. As resurrected Messiah, Jesus has the authority to bless" (Gaebelein, ed., *The Expositor's Bible Commentary,* Zondervan).

Jesus' ascension marks the end of His physical presence with the disciples. His work would continue in heaven as their (and our) Intercessor (Heb. 7:25; 9:24). The special work of the Holy Spirit would soon begin. The disciples were prepared for the Spirit's imminent coming, and He would prepare them fully for the task before them.

The disciples' worship (Luke 24:52-53). Jesus had now departed. Before, when Jesus had left them to be crucified and buried, His followers had lost all hope and secluded themselves in fear. When He departed for heaven this time, their reaction was very different. Now they had the hope Christ's resurrection brings, and they had a fuller understanding of all that had happened (cf. vs. 45).

As a result, the disciples "worshipped him, and returned to Jerusalem with great joy" (vs. 52). They were fully convinced not only of the resurrection but of Jesus' deity as well. This brought worship that expressed their inward joy. Their worship did not end on the Mount of Olives but continued in the temple as they praised God (vs. 53).

The resurrection is a past event, but it means that we can have the same joy today that it brought the first disciples. It gives us the assurance that the One we serve is the eternal God and that He has given us victory over death. He gives us eternal hope, a hope that looks beyond the sufferings and struggles of this life and gives us reason to rejoice.

—*Jarl K. Waggoner.*

PRACTICAL POINTS

1. When confusion or doubts arise, we need to focus on the hope we have through the resurrected Lord (Luke 24:36-43).
2. The Bible will be largely a mystery to us unless we see that all its parts point to Jesus Christ (vs. 44).
3. The Bible is a supernatural book that requires that we seek divine help in understanding it fully (vss. 45-46).
4. God's eternal plan includes us as the witnesses called to take the gospel to the world (vss. 47-48).
5. God has promised to give us the power we need to fulfill the role He has for us (vs. 49).
6. The work of Christ in the past, along with His present work, calls for our continual worship and praise of Him (vss. 50-53).

—*Jarl K. Waggoner.*

FOR DAILY MEDITATION

MONDAY, Apr. 10.   Acts 1:1-4.

Many infallible proofs. After His resurrection, Jesus not only appeared to His disciples on numerous occasions, but He also walked with two of them on the way from Jerusalem to Emmaus (cf. Luke 24:13-27), ate with them more than once (cf. vs. 30; vss. 41-43), cooked breakfast for them (cf. John 21:9-13), and even allowed them to examine His crucifixion wounds (cf. Luke 24:39-40; John 20:27).

TUESDAY, Apr. 11.   I Cor. 15:3-8.

Christ arose. Around A.D. 135, the emperor Hadrian, for the expressed purpose of quashing Christianity, covered the known historical sites of Christ's crucifixion and resurrection with a massive concrete platform and built a temple to Zeus on it. Two centuries later, when Constantine wanted to restore the sites for Christian worship by building churches to commemorate them, local Christians could just point him to Hadrian's temple as marking those locations.

WEDNESDAY, Apr. 12.
I John 1:1-4.

The Word of Life. John told his readers that he and his companions were those who had personally seen, heard, and touched the incarnate Word of God. John wanted to declare Jesus as the Word of eternal life to his readers so that their fellowship might be directly with God the Father and God the Son.

THURSDAY, Apr. 13.
Mark 16:12-14.

Jesus with the disciples. This is a summary of the events of Luke 24:13-49. But Mark's emphasis here is on the disciples' failure to believe that Jesus had risen from the dead. He focuses on Jesus as strongly rebuking their unbelief and hardness of heart.

FRIDAY, Apr. 14.   Luke 24:13-35.

The road to Emmaus. Cleopas and his companion were weighed down by the heartbreak and disappointment of Jesus' death. When their conversation reached the ears of a Stranger traveling the same road, He asked them why they were distressed. They were shocked that anyone by now would not have heard the sorrowful news of Jesus' crucifixion. They told Him how their hopes were dashed. The Stranger explained how Scripture testifies of Christ's triumph through His death and resurrection.

SATURDAY, Apr. 15.
John 21:1-14.

The third appearance. John was the first to recognize the Stranger on the shore that day as the risen Lord Jesus. Peter, ever the impulsive one, swam immediately to shore while the other disciples came in on a small boat with their miraculous catch of fish. As we mature in the Christian life through experience, we learn to recognize the Lord.

SUNDAY, Apr. 16.   Luke 24:36-53.

Scripture now fulfilled. Luke records that, just prior to His ascension into heaven, Jesus appeared among the disciples at Jerusalem while they were gathered together to hear the report of Cleopas and his companion. At that time, Jesus demonstrated irrefutably that His resurrection was physical by showing them His crucifixion wounds and by eating. This proof would become especially important in combatting the heresy of Gnosticism, which denied both the Lord's bodily resurrection, as well as His incarnation.

—*John Lody.*

SCRIPTURE LESSON TEXT

JOHN 6:22 The day following, when the people which stood on the other side of the sea saw that there was none other boat there, save that one whereinto his disciples were entered, and that Jesus went not with his disciples into the boat, but *that* his disciples were gone away alone;

23 (Howbeit there came other boats from Tiberias nigh unto the place where they did eat bread, after that the Lord had given thanks:)

24 When the people therefore saw that Jesus was not there, neither his disciples, they also took shipping, and came to Capernaum, seeking for Jesus.

25 And when they had found him on the other side of the sea, they said unto him, Rabbi, when camest thou hither?

26 Jesus answered them and said, Verily, verily, I say unto you, Ye seek me, not because ye saw the miracles, but because ye did eat of the loaves, and were filled.

27 Labour not for the meat which perisheth, but for that meat which endureth unto everlasting life, which the Son of man shall give unto you: for him hath God the Father sealed.

28 Then said they unto him, What shall we do, that we might work the works of God?

29 Jesus answered and said unto them, This is the work of God, that ye believe on him whom he hath sent.

30 They said therefore unto him, What sign shewest thou then, that we may see, and believe thee? what dost thou work?

31 Our fathers did eat manna in the desert; as it is written, He gave them bread from heaven to eat.

32 Then Jesus said unto them, Verily, verily, I say unto you, Moses gave you not that bread from heaven; but my Father giveth you the true bread from heaven.

33 For the bread of God is he which cometh down from heaven, and giveth life unto the world.

34 Then said they unto him, Lord, evermore give us this bread.

35 And Jesus said unto them, I am the bread of life: he that cometh to me shall never hunger; and he that believeth on me shall never thirst.

NOTES

The Bread of Life

Lesson Text: John 6:22-35

Related Scriptures: Exodus 16:4-18; Isaiah 55:1-7; John 6:1-13

TIME: A.D. 29   PLACE: Sea of Galilee

GOLDEN TEXT—"Jesus said unto them, I am the bread of life: he that cometh to me shall never hunger; and he that believeth on me shall never thirst" (John 6:35).

Lesson Exposition

Jesus and His disciples had been on the northeastern shore of the Sea of Galilee. There He fed the multitude. Afterward, the disciples took a ship during the night to Capernaum, on the western shore of the sea. They ran into a storm on their way. After Jesus walked on the water and joined them, they immediately arrived at their destination (John 6:9-21).

SEARCH FOR JESUS—John 6:22-24

The day following the miraculous feeding, the crowds had not returned to their homes. They realized that although the disciples had crossed over to Capernaum, Jesus had not embarked with them. Failing to find Him, they concluded that He was with His disciples, though they had no clue as to how He had made it to Capernaum. They crossed over to Capernaum on boats sent over from Tiberias, and their search for Jesus continued.

ENCOUNTERING JESUS—John 6:25-35

The dialogue between Jesus and the people who had followed Him took place in the synagogue in Capernaum (vs. 59).

Food that endures (John 6:25-27). When the people finally found Jesus at Capernaum, they asked Him when He had arrived since they had not seen Jesus leave with His disciples. Jesus' miracle walk on the water was a private miracle for His disciples only.

Jesus went to the heart of their search for Him by reprimanding them for their motive. The truth was that their quest was not precipitated by an understanding of the messianic significance of the miracle feeding. Their interest was only in keeping their stomachs filled. They were concerned with the here and now.

Jesus led them in a spiritual direction by telling them that they should not labor for physical bread that perishes. They instead were to seek the true Bread that endures to everlasting life. The Son of Man is the true Bread, which does not perish. The Father has certified the Son as the Provider of eternal life by His miracles (Acts 2:22; cf. John 3:2; 4:48; 10:38; Acts 10:38).

Faith required (John 6:28-29). The people then wanted to know what they needed to do in order to win God's favor. They interpreted Christ's words as indicating that certain works would earn God's salvation. This implied a sense of self-sufficiency, as though humans were capable of doing the works of God.

Jesus responded that God required only one thing. They must believe in Christ, whom God had sent to them. This was very stunning to those caught up in law keeping in hopes of meeting God's demands. Faith in Christ is not a work (cf. 3:16), for salvation is not the result of doing good works (Eph. 2:8-9). Salvation is the free gift of God (Rom. 6:23).

True Bread from heaven (John 6:30-33). The crowd asked Jesus for an authenticating sign of His authority (cf. 2:18). They wanted something that they could see; then they would believe Jesus' words. This was an incredible request, for they had just participated in the miraculous multiplication of the bread and fish. They used Moses as an example of what they wanted to see. They believed he had given them manna from heaven, which authenticated him (Ex. 16:4, 15).

Jesus responded that it was the Father who had given them the manna from heaven. He was now giving them the true Bread from heaven, which satisfies permanently. The manna provided physical nourishment only. The true Bread from heaven is a necessity for eternal life. Jesus is the true Bread who came down from heaven to give life to those who partake of it (John 6:51).

Bread of Life (John 6:34-35). The people, addressing Jesus as "Lord," asked Him to give them bread from heaven from now on. They wanted a continuing supply that would never fail. Due to their materialistic mindset, they still did not understand that Christ was speaking of the spiritual bread that provides eternal life.

Jesus identified Himself as the Bread of Life. The Bread was a Person, not a commodity (vs. 33). "I am" (vs. 35) is one of several "I am" revelations in John (cf. 8:12; 15:1). Those who come to Him in faith shall never hunger. He imparts and sustains spiritual life. They do not need to receive the Bread of Life repeatedly. Spiritual thirst is quenched forever through faith in Him.

"Jesus had already startled people by saying that Moses did not give them real bread from heaven. Now he shocked them a second time by announcing he was the bread the Father had given. Jesus claimed to be the only permanent satisfaction for the human desire for life" (Gaebelein, ed., *The Expositor's Bible Commentary,* Zondervan).

—*Jack Riggs.*

PRACTICAL POINTS

1. People will often go to great lengths to find Jesus for whatever reason (John 6:22-24).

2. Jesus knows the desires and motives of people's hearts when they come to Him (vss. 25-26).

3. The real values of life are those that have eternal value (vs. 27).

4. People often want to follow their own way to please God rather than His (vss. 28-29).

5. Some people want to test God before deciding whether they will believe Him (vss. 30-31).

6. Jesus is God's only provision for men to have eternal life (vss. 32-33).

7. Only Christ can satisfy completely the spiritual hunger and thirst of man's heart (vss. 34-35).

—*Jack Riggs.*

FOR DAILY MEDITATION

MONDAY, Apr. 17.   John 6:1-13.
The feeding of the five thousand. As the disciples handed out the small amount of food to those who were seated, more loaves kept coming, and more fishes too! It must have been perplexing for the Twelve; every time they thought they must have just given out the last of the food, there was always more to give! So it is with God's generosity. The more generous we are to others, the more we experience just how limitless His generosity really is!

TUESDAY, Apr. 18.   Ex. 16:4-18.
God sends manna. It had been a month and a half since the Israelites had left Egypt, and they were hungry. They began their familiar refrain, accusing Moses of bringing them out into the wilderness, merely to die. Yet Yahweh overlooked their lack of gratitude and miraculously provided them with abundant bread every morning and abundant quail every evening. Give thanks today for God's forbearance and generosity to His people.

WEDNESDAY, Apr. 19.
Num. 11:4-10.
Complaints about manna. Suddenly, slavery in Egypt had become something close to paradise in the imaginations of the Israelites. They actually stood at the doors of their tents weeping, missing the sumptuous cuisine they remembered having in Egypt. What complaints in your own life might be displeasing to the Lord?

THURSDAY, Apr. 20.   Ps. 78:17-31.
Judgment for ungrateful hearts. The ingratitude of the Israelites provoked the Lord's wrath. He would give them just what they asked for: meat. In fact, they would have so much meat to eat that it would be coming out of their ears! But before they had finished even their first meal of it, they would also receive judgment for their ingratitude. Their young men would die by a plague sent from the Lord. Sometimes God grants us things we should not have asked for to teach us how wrong our desires really are.

FRIDAY, Apr. 21.   Isa. 55:1-7.
God's mercy on mankind. When Jesus said, "Blessed are they which do hunger and thirst after righteousness: for they shall be filled" (Matt. 5:6), He was likely alluding to this very prophecy by Isaiah. All of Jesus' miracles involving food and drink were illustrations to help people understand the spiritual reality of God's provision of righteousness for their salvation from sin. But the dullness of their hearts led most of them to follow Him around, hoping for little more than another free meal.

SATURDAY, Apr. 22.
John 6:47-58.
One with Christ. On the surface, to eat Jesus' flesh and to drink His blood sounds like an unsavory prospect. But Jesus was driving home the spiritual truth that, in order to partake of His gift of eternal life, we must make the offering of His flesh and blood for our sins our essential spiritual diet. Nothing else is worthy to trust for our sustenance.

SUNDAY, Apr. 23.   John 6:22-35.
The true Bread from heaven. Jesus' interchange with the multitude that followed Him to Capernaum from the east side of Galilee is a verbal joust where each party keeps talking past the other. Jesus speaks on a spiritual level, but the crowd keeps trying to get Him to give them more free food. Trading spiritual riches for earthly gain leaves the trader bankrupt in the end.
—*John Lody.*

SCRIPTURE LESSON TEXT

JOHN 8:12 Then spake Jesus again unto them, saying, I am the light of the world: he that followeth me shall not walk in darkness, but shall have the light of life.

13 The Pharisees therefore said unto him, Thou bearest record of thyself; thy record is not true.

14 Jesus answered and said unto them, Though I bear record of myself, *yet* my record is true: for I know whence I came, and whither I go; but ye cannot tell whence I come, and whither I go.

15 Ye judge after the flesh; I judge no man.

16 And yet if I judge, my judgment is true: for I am not alone, but I and the Father that sent me.

17 It is also written in your law, that the testimony of two men is true.

18 I am one that bear witness of myself, and the Father that sent me beareth witness of me.

19 Then said they unto him, Where is thy Father? Jesus answered, Ye neither know me, nor my Father: if ye had known me, ye should have known my Father also.

20 These words spake Jesus in the treasury, as he taught in the temple: and no man laid hands on him; for his hour was not yet come.

12:44 Jesus cried and said, He that believeth on me, believeth not on me, but on him that sent me.

45 And he that seeth me seeth him that sent me.

46 I am come a light into the world, that whosoever believeth on me should not abide in darkness.

NOTES

The Light of the World

Lesson Text: John 8:12-20; 12:44-46

Related Scriptures: Isaiah 9:2-6; Matthew 5:14-16;
John 1:1-10; I John 5:5-13

TIMES: A.D. 29; 30   PLACE: Jerusalem

GOLDEN TEXT—"I am the light of the world: he that followeth me shall not walk in darkness, but shall have the light of life" (John 8:12).

Lesson Exposition

Our lesson this week teaches us how Jesus supports and sustains us by showing us that He is the Light of the World. In a world of spiritual darkness, we need the true Light that dispels the darkness of ignorance and sin and shows us the way.

JESUS IS THE LIGHT OF THE WORLD—John 8:12-20

A unique claim (John 8:12). When Jesus began His public ministry, the small town of Nazareth did not know what to make of Him. Then He started making many claims like the ones we saw last week, claims that He was the Bread of Life and the Living Water. This astounded the people even more. This week, we see how Jesus made the unique claim to be the Light of the World.

Jesus came to point people to heaven, and He promised that He was indeed the way to God. He was also the Light that showed the way to God. When one follows the true Light, there is no possibility that one will stumble in the darkness. Surrounded by a world with conflicting opinions about the truth, we have Jesus, who is not only the way to God but also the Light that illuminates our path.

Jesus' claim was true, for there was no darkness in Him. Never in history has anyone else who made similar claims ever backed them up with deeds. All would-be saviors or messiahs before and after Him have been charlatans who fell short of the true Light of the World. In this respect, Jesus is indeed unique, for there is only one Saviour for this world, and His light dispels the darkness. When we follow Jesus, we cannot ever go wrong, for He is the only true way to heaven.

Response to criticism (John 8:13-18). Jesus was fully aware of the criticism and skepticism that surrounded the claims He made. He sought to calm the people's fears. After all, they thought that He was just a carpenter's son from Nazareth.

Jesus was fully aware that He was making these claims about Himself. He told the people so. He also explained that He knew where He came from and where He was going. They could not understand that. Jesus knew both with absolute certainty.

When Jesus was on earth, He came

44

as Saviour and not as Judge. His hearers were judging Him with human limitations. According to the law, witnesses were important for credibility. Jesus said that both He and His Father were adequate witnesses to the truth of what He taught and claimed. We can trust Him.

Jesus' heavenly Father (John 8:19-20). The people wanted more answers. They questioned His heritage and asked about His father. They were obviously thinking in earthly terms. Jesus had far more to offer. He sought to help them think His thoughts. Jesus told them that if they knew Him, they would automatically know who His Father is. They were interrelated. One could not be known without the other. Jesus was one with the Father.

It is interesting that Jesus spoke these words in a public place. He spoke in the temple courts at Jerusalem. But it was not yet God's appointed time for further developments to happen, so the people did not dare lay hands on Him and take Him in.

The lesson for us here is that we must realize that knowing Jesus is the way to know God the Father. Jesus is the only light that we will ever need in our journey to God.

THE CONSEQUENCES OF FOLLOWING THE TRUE LIGHT— John 12:44-46

Regarding Jesus' statement in verse 44, William Hendriksen gave this insight: "As more often in statements of this nature (see on 4:21; 12:30) the sense is: 'He who believes in me does not exclusively believe in me but believes also in him who sent me'" (*New Testament Commentary,* Baker).

Jesus was bringing His point home to a crowd that was resistant to the truth of the gospel. They were steeped in unbelief. Jesus told them that He was there in front of them and that

when they saw Him, they were looking at the Father. Jesus is the God-Man. He is God in the flesh come to earth. Those who choose to put their trust in Jesus, the Light, will never walk in darkness again, for He is their light.

Jesus then told them that those who choose not to obey Him will be judged by the Father. Jesus came to prevent that and to lead people home. The truth of Jesus' message will be made clear in the end times. Jesus spoke according to the Father's instructions, and those instructions lead to eternal life.

We too are called to follow the light of Jesus, which leads us to our heavenly home. We must continually increase in godly virtues (II Pet. 1:5-9). If we do not, we become shortsighted and blind and return to the darkness of sin that leads to death.

—A. Koshy Muthalaly.

PRACTICAL POINTS

1. If we follow Jesus, we will not stumble in the darkness but have the light that leads to life (John 8:12).
2. Jesus is the only one who knows the way (vss. 13-14).
3. Jesus' claims are sufficient for us, for we know truly that the Father has sent Him to us (vss. 15-18).
4. When we come to know Jesus, we get to know God the Father as well (vss. 19-20).
5. When we trust Jesus, we can be sure we are trusting the same God who sent Jesus to us (12:44).
6. When we see the works and wonders of Jesus, we see God (vs. 45).
7. If we trust Jesus, who is the Light, we will always walk in the light that He provides us (vs. 46).

—A. Koshy Muthalaly.

FOR DAILY MEDITATION

MONDAY, Apr. 24.   Isa. 9:2-4.

A Light to the nations. Isaiah 9 is a messianic prophecy that was fulfilled when the glory of the Son of God was revealed to the towns on shores of the sea of Galilee as He began preaching there. The glory that Jesus revealed to the world during His earthly ministry was not the temporary glory of the old covenant, the bright but fading light that shone from Moses' face after he had met with the Lord (cf. Ex. 34:29-30; II Cor. 3:7-14). Jesus' glory was perfect holiness, love, compassion, and truth.

TUESDAY, Apr. 25.   John 1:1-10.

The true Light. Even though Jesus is the Creator of the world, when He came into the world, the world refused to recognize Him. They were too busy suppressing the truth. To acknowledge that Jesus is the Way, the Truth, and the Life would entail facing up to their lost condition before God. That would require the Holy Spirit intervening with grace and the gift of saving faith (cf. Eph. 2:8-9).

WEDNESDAY, Apr. 26.
Phil. 2:12-16.

Believers shine forth in the world. Paul's words are relevant for our present situation. As the world becomes increasingly perverse and rebellious against God, we must guard against becoming discouraged from maintaining our faithfulness and obedience to God so that our witness will shine forth in the darkness as God intends (vs. 15). At the same time, we must not allow our pursuit of true holiness to become twisted into a repulsive, judgmental self-righteousness that alienates us from the society around us.

THURSDAY, Apr. 27.
I John 5:5-13.

Life through the Son. John was most likely rebuking a heresy called Docetism, which taught that Jesus was a mere man who only became the Son of God at His baptism when the Holy Spirit descended upon Him. It also taught that Jesus ceased to be the Son of God when the Holy Spirit (supposedly) departed from Him just before His death on the cross. For John, the testimony of the water and the blood were of the utmost importance in proving that Jesus is fully human and that He truly died (cf. John 19:33-37).

FRIDAY, Apr. 28.   John 3:16-21.

Out of the darkness into the light. After telling Nicodemus how God loved the world so much that He sent His Son to save it and not to condemn it, Jesus went on to say a lot about condemnation. None of us would ever come to Jesus in our fallen state. Christ's light reveals our guilt!

SATURDAY, Apr. 29.
Prov. 4:14-22.

The path of the just. The difference between the darkness in lives of wicked people and the shining light that grows ever brighter in lives of the righteous is the Word of God. Those who hear and obey the Father's Word will keep themselves walking in the light.

SUNDAY, Apr. 30.
John 8:12-20; 12:44-46.

The Light of Life. Often in the Gospels, Jesus spoke to His audience (in this instance the Pharisees) on a spiritual level, while those in His audience spoke and thought merely on an earthly one. Although Jesus always bore witness of Himself and His heavenly Father, His hearers remained confused and unable to get to the true meaning of what He was saying.

—John Lody.

Scripture Lesson Text

JOHN 10:7 Then said Jesus unto them again, Verily, verily, I say unto you, I am the door of the sheep.

8 All that ever came before me are thieves and robbers: but the sheep did not hear them.

9 I am the door: by me if any man enter in, he shall be saved, and shall go in and out, and find pasture.

10 The thief cometh not, but for to steal, and to kill, and to destroy: I am come that they might have life, and that they might have *it* more abundantly.

11 I am the good shepherd: the good shepherd giveth his life for the sheep.

12 But he that is an hireling, and not the shepherd, whose own the sheep are not, seeth the wolf coming, and leaveth the sheep, and fleeth: and the wolf catcheth them, and scattereth the sheep.

13 The hireling fleeth, because he is an hireling, and careth not for the sheep.

14 I am the good shepherd, and know my *sheep,* and am known of mine.

15 As the Father knoweth me, even so know I the Father: and I lay down my life for the sheep.

16 And other sheep I have, which are not of this fold: them also I must bring, and they shall hear my voice; and there shall be one fold, *and* one shepherd.

17 Therefore doth my Father love me, because I lay down my life, that I might take it again.

18 No man taketh it from me, but I lay it down of myself. I have power to lay it down, and I have power to take it again. This commandment have I received of my Father.

NOTES

The Good Shepherd

Lesson Text: John 10:7-18

Related Scriptures: Psalm 23:1-6; Jeremiah 23:1-6;
Ezekiel 34:10-25; I Peter 5:1-4

TIME: A.D. 29   PLACE: Jerusalem

GOLDEN TEXT—"I am the good shepherd: the good shepherd giveth his life for the sheep" (John 10:11).

Lesson Exposition

Jesus used the analogy of the sheepfold and the shepherd to illustrate His special relationship with believers. As the Door, He is their access to security and spiritual nourishment. As the Good Shepherd, He is their Provider, Guide, and Protector.

THE DOOR OF THE SHEEPFOLD—John 10:7-10

The Door (John 10:7-8). The sheepfold was located near the pasture where the sheep found nourishment. The shepherd stood at the door of the fold to allow the sheep to go in and out. Jesus is the Door for His sheep, His disciples. The religious leaders who came before Him (Matt. 23:13-15) were like thieves and robbers. They cared little for the spiritual well-being of Israel. (False leaders are the same today.) Christ's sheep did not listen to them.

Abundant life (John 10:9-10). As the Door, Jesus is the exclusive entrance for His flock (14:6). Those who enter through Him receive eternal life and salvation (3:16-17). Christ provides them with spiritual nourishment and safety (Ps. 23:2). While the reli-

gious leadership steal, kill, and destroy people spiritually (Matt. 23:15), Christ gives eternal life in abundance to His sheep (John 4:14).

THE GOOD SHEPHERD SAVES HIS SHEEP—John 10:11-13

Christ is the Good Shepherd. The word "good" means of high moral value (cf. 14:11). He is the only one in His class. He showed His excellence by giving His life for the sheep.

The life of the shepherd is one of potential danger (cf. I Sam. 17:34-35, 37) due to the predatory animals on the prowl. Jesus did not risk His life to save His sheep from danger. He deliberately laid His life down willingly on behalf of the sheep (Gal. 1:4; Eph. 5:2). Jesus substituted His life for theirs (I Pet. 2:24; 3:18).

If an ordinary shepherd died risking his life to protect the sheep, the flock would be scattered and lost. But Jesus' death brought life for the sheep. They were in danger of perishing, but by His death He saved them. Believers are His sheep, whom He purchased with His blood (Acts 20:28).

In stark contrast to Jesus were

the religious leaders. They were like hired hands, who do not have the same commitment to the well-being of the sheep as the shepherd. When the wolves come, they abandon the flock for their own safety. The sheep are left to be violently abused and scattered.

THE GOOD SHEPHERD KNOWS HIS SHEEP—John 10:14-18

Mutual knowledge (John 10:14-15). The Good Shepherd knows His sheep by experience. Christ has an intimate and personal relationship with believers. The relationship is reciprocal, for they know Him. This is evident in their hearing His voice and following Him (vs. 27).

The intimacy between the Shepherd and His sheep reflects the intimate relationship of the Father and the Son. Christ and the Father are one (10:30; 14:7, 10-11). They are one in essence, mind, purpose, and works. Jesus' voluntary and sacrificial death was necessary for Him and His sheep to know one another intimately.

Other sheep (John 10:16). Christ has other sheep whom He will bring into the fold. These are the Gentiles who listen to His voice. He will shepherd the one flock, the church made up of Jewish and Gentile believers (Eph. 3:6).

Divine destiny (John 10:17-18). The Father has a special love for the Son because He laid down His life in order to take it up again. Christ's resurrection was not an afterthought.

No one took Jesus' life from Him. There were failed attempts on His life (5:18; 8:59), but He laid His life down voluntarily. He was not a martyr, nor was His death an accident. He was in complete charge (Luke 23:46). Christ had sovereign authority over His own destiny. He had the right to lay down

His life and to take it up again.

Christ's death would have no saving value if it had not been voluntary. He was commissioned by the Father to do what He did (John 12:49-50; 14:31). Nothing was outside of the Father's plan.

"The death of Jesus, though voluntary, was not merely assent to being killed, a sort of indirect suicide; it was part of a plan to submit to death and then emerge from it victoriously alive. Anyone can lay down his life, if that means simply the termination of physical existence; but only the Son of the Father could at will resume his existence. He was acting in accord with a divine plan that involved a supreme sacrifice and a manifestation of divine power" (Gaebelein, ed., *The Expositor's Bible Commentary,* Zondervan).

—*Jack Riggs.*

PRACTICAL POINTS

1. Christ is the only access we have into the salvation and abundant life of His flock (John 10:7-10).

2. Christ's sacrificial death contradicts the idea that salvation is by good works (vs. 11).

3. As our Good Shepherd, Christ will never abandon us in the face of spiritual danger (vss. 12-13).

4. Jesus knows each of us personally in the loving and caring relationship He has with all believers (vss. 14-15).

5. Christ's death is sufficient to save all those who trust in Him (vs. 16).

6. The love and sovereign power of God were both displayed in Christ's death for sinners (vss. 17-18).

—*Jack Riggs.*

FOR DAILY MEDITATION

MONDAY, May 1. Ps. 23:1-6.

The Lord is my Shepherd. This psalm is obviously broader in scope than just a testimony of David about his experience of God as his Shepherd. It is, of course, a messianic prophecy. It is also a foreshadowing of Jesus' discourse about Himself in John 10:7-18. Further, it is the testimony of every heart that has been saved by the grace of the Good Shepherd.

TUESDAY, May 2. Ezek. 34:10-25.

The Lord's flock. On one level, Ezekiel is prophesying against the evil shepherds of Israel, who are exploiting the people and taking all the riches and the resources of the land for themselves, leaving nothing but the dregs for everyone else. God promises to bring justice to His exploited people and to punish all those who have deliberately impoverished them. But on a more profound level, this is a prophecy of Messiah as the Good Shepherd who will one day gather all His people for whom He laid down His life.

**WEDNESDAY, May 3.
John 21:15-17.**

Peter commissioned to shepherd. Peter denied Jesus before witnesses three times on the night of His betrayal. The one who had vowed to follow Him, even if it meant death, could not even bring himself to admit to knowing Jesus. Here Jesus offered Peter the chance to repent of his three denials by thrice professing his love for Him. But Jesus required more. Peter must prove his love by devoting his life to the care of Jesus' disciples. This is the proof of our love for Christ—that we feed His sheep

THURSDAY, May 4.   I Pet. 5:1-4.

Shepherd the flock. Peter passed along the charge that Jesus gave to him: "Feed my sheep" (John 21:16-17). But he cautioned that the role of shepherd should not be undertaken for the wrong reasons—not out of obligation or pressure, not for material gain, and not to wield power over others. A shepherd of God's flock should serve out of love for the Lord and His people, with a heartfelt eagerness to impart God's truth for their good.

FRIDAY, May 5.   Isa. 40:9-14.

He will feed His flock. This is the source for the popular segment, "O thou that tellest good tidings to Zion" in Handel's *Messiah.* Even though Jesus is described as coming in divine might and authority, His role as a gentle shepherd is emphasized. With all the sovereign power of His deity, Jesus came as a loving shepherd to gather lost sinners to Himself with patience for their human frailty.

SATURDAY, May 6.   Heb. 13:20-21.

Perfect in every good work. This is the closing doxology of the epistle to the Hebrews. Normally considered a humble or even disreputable vocation in other contexts, the role of shepherd is elevated to divine status. For Christians, the Great Shepherd is the Lord and Saviour of those who are supremely blessed to be His humble sheep.

SUNDAY, May 7.   John 10:7-18.

The Door to eternal life. Before the true Door to the sheep came, there had been many false shepherds, but the Father's sheep did not hear them. They were awaiting the true voice of the Good Shepherd, who would lay down His very life for them. Praise the Lord for His gracious deliverance in your life today!

—*John Lody.*

SCRIPTURE LESSON TEXT

JOHN 11:17 Then when Jesus came, he found that he had *lain* in the grave four days already.

18 Now Bethany was nigh unto Jerusalem, about fifteen furlongs off:

19 And many of the Jews came to Martha and Mary, to comfort them concerning their brother.

20 Then Martha, as soon as she heard that Jesus was coming, went and met him: but Mary sat *still* in the house.

21 Then said Martha unto Jesus, Lord, if thou hadst been here, my brother had not died.

22 But I know, that even now, whatsoever thou wilt ask of God, God will give *it* thee.

23 Jesus saith unto her, Thy brother shall rise again.

24 Martha saith unto him, I know that he shall rise again in the resurrection at the last day.

25 Jesus said unto her, I am the resurrection, and the life: he that believeth in me, though he were dead, yet shall he live:

26 And whosoever liveth and believeth in me shall never die. Believest thou this?

27 She saith unto him, Yea, Lord: I believe that thou art the Christ, the Son of God, which should come into the world.

NOTES

The Resurrection and the Life

Lesson Text: John 11:17-27

Related Scriptures: Daniel 12:1-3; John 11:1-16, 28-45;
I Corinthians 15:20-26; Philippians 3:7-14

TIME: A.D. 30   PLACE: Bethany

GOLDEN TEXT—"I am the resurrection, and the life: he that believeth in me, though he were dead, yet shall he live" (John 11:25).

Lesson Exposition

Lazarus was ill (John 11:1-3). His sisters, Mary and Martha, sent a messenger to notify Jesus. Jesus responded that death would not be the final outcome of Lazarus's sickness (vs. 4). Christ would manifest the glory of God.

Two days later, Jesus told His disciples that Lazarus was dead (vss. 6, 11-14) but that He was going to awaken Lazarus out of the sleep of death. Jesus would demonstrate that He was the Resurrection and the Life in order to strengthen the faith of the disciples, family members, and friends.

ARRIVAL OF JESUS—
John 11:17-20

The delay (John 11:17-18). Lazarus lived with his sisters in Bethany, which was about two miles east of Jerusalem. When Jesus arrived, He found that Lazarus had been in the grave four days. It would have required the messenger one day to have reached Jesus from Bethany, since He was beyond the Jordan River on the east side (10:40). Jesus' trip to Bethany would have taken one day. In addition, Jesus waited two days

before He began His journey (11:6).

After four days in the grave, there would be no doubt that Lazarus had died. The warm Palestinian climate would have quickly caused the onset of decomposition (vs. 39). Burials were usually on the day of death (Acts 5:6, 10). Jesus delayed not as a matter of hard-heartedness but rather to prepare the stage for God's glory to be manifested.

Martha met Jesus (John 11:19-20). The social standing of the family was probably the reason so many Jews were engaged in the pious duty of comforting the bereaved. Martha went out to meet Jesus, while her sister, Mary, remained seated in the home as she received mourners.

ANNOUNCEMENT OF JESUS—
John 11:21-24

Martha's request (John 11:21-22). Martha expressed her faith in the midst of her grief. If Jesus had been there, her brother would have been healed. She was not criticizing Jesus for His absence. Lazarus had probably died the same day that the messenger was sent to Jesus.

Martha told Jesus she believed that God would grant Him whatever He asked of the Father. She was asking Jesus to raise her brother right then. She possibly had heard of Jesus' response that Lazarus's sickness was "not unto death" (vs. 4). Martha either had not heard or at least understood the words "for the glory of God."

Jesus' prophecy (John 11:23-24). Jesus assured Martha that Lazarus would rise from the dead. Martha responded by affirming her confident belief that Lazarus would be in the final resurrection at the last day. She believed in the Old Testament hope (Job 19:25-27; Dan. 12:2) as well as in the promise of Christ Himself (John 5:28-29). But Martha had missed the point. Jesus was about to raise Lazarus immediately.

ASSERTION OF JESUS— John 11:25-27

Resurrection and life (John 11:25-26). Jesus directed Martha's faith to personal faith in Him. He declared, "I am the resurrection, and the life." The source of both the resurrection and eternal life resides in Christ (Rom. 6:8-9; I Cor. 15:20). He has the power to raise the dead. He gives and sustains eternal life to believers.

Christ instructed Martha further. The believer who dies has the hope of the resurrection. His physical death is not final (I Thess. 4:16). Those who live and believe will never die. They live by faith and will never die spiritually (John 6:47).

Jesus asked Martha whether she believed this. Did she have a personal trust in Him as the source of the resurrection and of eternal life? Christ was going to provide a resurrection in the here and now by raising Lazarus as a pattern of the final resurrection to

come. "For the heathen or the unbeliever death may be thought of as the end. Not so for the man who believes in Christ. Such a man may die in the sense that he passes through the door we call physical death, but he will not die in the fuller sense. Death for him is but the gateway to further life and fellowship with God" (Morris, *The Gospel According to John,* Eerdmans).

Martha's confession (John 11:27). Martha confessed, "Yea, Lord: I believe." This had a settled conviction. She believed that Jesus was the Messiah, the Son of God (cf. 20:31). She believed He had come into the world to do what He chose to do. He came to do the Father's will (John 6:38; cf. Matt. 26:39; John 3:17).

—*Jack Riggs.*

PRACTICAL POINTS

1. God accomplishes His merciful purpose on His own timetable to fit His specific plan (John 11:17-18).

2. The difficult times of life are times in which we must place our trust in God's will (vss. 19-21).

3. No matter how hard a situation may be, there is always hope in Christ (vss. 22-23).

4. God's promises for the future never change despite the trials of today (vs. 24).

5. Only Christ can guarantee hope beyond the grave (vs. 25).

6. Our doubts and fears are removed when we focus on Christ, who provides and sustains our eternal life (vs. 26).

7. We should affirm our faith in Christ without reservation (vs. 27).

—*Jack Riggs.*

FOR DAILY MEDITATION

MONDAY, May 8.   John 11:1-16.

The death of Lazarus. Jesus loved Mary, Martha, and their sick brother Lazarus, but "he abode two days still in the same place where he was" (vs. 6). What a strange way to behave when you hear of a friend in need! But God's ways are not our ways (cf. Isa. 55:8-9). While Mary, Martha, and His disciples were undoubtedly perplexed by Jesus' lack of action on Lazarus's behalf, He had everything under His sovereign control.

TUESDAY, May 9.   John 11:28-45.

Lazarus raised to life. When Jesus wept, the responses of those gathered were mixed. Some were touched by Jesus' tears over the death of His good friend and the agonized grief of his sisters. Others were critical; they were bewildered at Jesus' failure to prevent Lazarus's death when He had healed so many others. Once Jesus had raised Lazarus back to life and health, however, they changed their tune and believed in Him. We must trust Him, even when what He is doing makes no sense to us.

**WEDNESDAY, May 10.
Dan. 12:1-3.**

Awakening to life or to shame. Daniel's vision was of an unprecedented time of trouble coming upon Israel, followed by the glorious deliverance of those whose names are written in God's book of life (cf. Phil. 4:3; Rev. 3:5; 13:8; 17:8; 20:12, 15; 21:27; 22:19). If your name is in that book, give thanks for God's gracious deliverance.

**THURSDAY, May 11.
I Cor. 15:20-26.**

The resurrection of the dead. Paul's point is plain. Since Christ rose from the dead, all those who are in Him will be raised at His return. Adam's sin brought death upon us all, but Christ's perfect sin offering brings life to the dead. Christ will reign until all powers are conquered and vanquished. Then every knee will bow and every mouth will confess that He is King of kings and Lord of Lords.

FRIDAY, May 12.   Phil. 3:7-14.

The power of His resurrection. Paul's confession is both dramatic and radical. All he had ever accomplished before he came to Christ and all he had lost because of his commitment to Christ he counted merely as detestable filth. Paul found the pearl of great price from Jesus' parable. Jesus is not something we merely add to our lives; He must become all that we live for!

**SATURDAY, May 13.
Acts 24:10-21.**

The resurrection of the just and unjust. The high priest used the same tactics against Paul as he had against Jesus—false charges of desecrating the temple and inciting a riot. Paul focused his defense on the future resurrection of the righteous and the wicked, hoping for a chance to preach the gospel to Felix. Paul eventually got his chance, but Felix was only interested in a bribe (cf. vs. 26). We cannot control how our witness will be received; our duty to the Lord is to witness faithfully.

SUNDAY, May 14.   John 11:17-27.

Those in Christ will never die. As steadfast as Martha's faith was, she still misunderstood Jesus' intentions for Lazarus. She did not expect Jesus to raise Lazarus from the dead, although there may be a veiled hope of it in her assertion, "But I know, that even now, whatsoever thou wilt ask of God, God will give it thee" (vs. 22). Jesus assures that believers will never die.
—John Lody.

SCRIPTURE LESSON TEXT

JOHN 15:1 I am the true vine, and my Father is the husbandman.

2 Every branch in me that beareth not fruit he taketh away: and every _branch_ that beareth fruit, he purgeth it, that it may bring forth more fruit.

3 Now ye are clean through the word which I have spoken unto you.

4 Abide in me, and I in you. As the branch cannot bear fruit of itself, except it abide in the vine; no more can ye, except ye abide in me.

5 I am the vine, ye _are_ the branches: He that abideth in me, and I in him, the same bringeth forth much fruit: for without me ye can do nothing.

6 If a man abide not in me, he is cast forth as a branch, and is withered; and men gather them, and cast _them_ into the fire, and they are burned.

7 If ye abide in me, and my words abide in you, ye shall ask what ye will, and it shall be done unto you.

8 Herein is my Father glorified, that ye bear much fruit; so shall ye be my disciples.

9 As the Father hath loved me, so have I loved you: continue ye in my love.

10 If ye keep my commandments, ye shall abide in my love; even as I have kept my Father's commandments, and abide in his love.

11 These things have I spoken unto you, that my joy might remain in you, and _that_ your joy might be full.

12 This is my commandment, That ye love one another, as I have loved you.

13 Greater love hath no man than this, that a man lay down his life for his friends.

14 Ye are my friends, if ye do whatsoever I command you.

15 Henceforth I call you not servants; for the servant knoweth not what his lord doeth: but I have called you friends; for all things that I have heard of my Father I have made known unto you.

16 Ye have not chosen me, but I have chosen you, and ordained you, that ye should go and bring forth fruit, and _that_ your fruit should remain: that whatsoever ye shall ask of the Father in my name, he may give it you.

17 These things I command you, that ye love one another.

NOTES

The True Vine

Lesson Text: John 15:1-17

Related Scriptures: Isaiah 5:1-7; 27:2-6; Colossians 2:6-10; I John 2:24-29

TIME: A.D. 30   PLACE: Jerusalem

GOLDEN TEXT—"I am the vine, ye are the branches: He that abideth in me, and I in him, the same bringeth forth much fruit: for without me ye can do nothing" (John 15:5).

Lesson Exposition

The secret of the Christian life is to stay close to Jesus. We dare not think that we can even try to follow the path of the cross without the life of Jesus flowing through us. On that day when Jesus died on the cross, the disciples felt abandoned. Their Master was gone, and they thought there was no more hope left. When Jesus rose again, the hope returned, for He is now with us always through His Holy Spirit.

JESUS IS THE TRUE VINE—
John 15:1-8

Remain in Jesus (John 15:1-4). The mark of a Christian disciple is the fruit he produces. Christians are to produce fruit. In order for fruit to appear, they are to stay close to Christ.

Jesus said that He is the true Vine and His Father is the gardener. Gardeners tend the vines and prune them when needed so that they will bear more fruit. God does that to us when we seek to follow Him. Our faith is often tested so that we know where we are in our relationship with Jesus. When we read the Word of God, we are encouraged toward greater produce. We have to stay close to the Vine in order to bear fruit.

Jesus reminds us that when we are separated from Him during those spiritually dry times when we do not read our Bibles or listen to Him, we cannot produce fruit. Spiritual fruit bearing is the result of careful nurture and staying close to Jesus.

True disciples produce fruit (John 15:5-8). Jesus said that He is the Vine and we are the branches. If we stay close to Him, we will be able to produce fruit. We cannot produce anything without Jesus, for He is our source of nourishment. When we think that we do not need Jesus and are self-sufficient, we can be sure that our downfall is not far away. Those who live apart from Jesus are like a branch that has dried up because it is not connected with the main vine. It will be thrown away, for it is useless.

There is another option. When we stay close to Jesus, the Vine, and keep His words in our hearts, we have the authority to ask for our needs in faith, and they will be granted to us. We have this power only when we abide close to Jesus. The mark of a true disciple is that he bears fruit and in so doing honors God the Father. We are called to bear much fruit and bring glory to God in what we do.

STAY CLOSE TO JESUS—
John 15:9-17

Love and obey Jesus (John 15:9-11). The true disciple seeks to please his Master. Jesus was loved by His Father, and He loves us the same way. Obedience to Jesus is a clear sign that we love Him just as Jesus obeyed His Father. We stay in His love by continuing to obey. When we disobey, we fall out of love with our Lord. Obedience and love go hand in hand. This is the secret to overflowing joy in the Christian life. Jesus set the example for this by obeying His heavenly Father.

Love others (John 15:12-13). Jesus gave us a command to love others just as He loves us. There is no Christian faith without love. The apostle John reminds us that if we do not love others, we do not know God (I John 4:8). Note that we are to love others in the same way that He loves us. We would be wise to identify in our own minds what characterizes Jesus' love for us, for that will clearly define for us how we are to love others.

Jesus went on to explain that the greatest love is that which is marked by the sacrifice of laying down one's life for one's friends. Jesus did exactly that for us. He died on the cross for us so that we could have eternal life.

Obedience makes us friends of Jesus (John 15:14-17). We do not usually associate obedience with friendship. Jesus puts that down as a requirement. We show that we are friends of Jesus by doing what He tells us. Friends are unlike servants, for friends share everything with one another as Jesus does with us—even all that He knows from the Father. Jesus chose us for friendship even when we rejected Him.

Jesus handpicked us to go out and bear fruit for Him. Now we have the privilege of receiving what we ask for because of the name of Jesus. "In telling the disciples to abide in him (verses 1-11), and especially in reminding them of his great elective love for them (the immediate context . . .), [Jesus] had one great purpose in mind, namely, 'in order that you may keep on loving one another.' The logic here is simple and clear. I, being in myself unlovable, cannot keep on loving my brother, who also is often very unlovable (at least as I see him), unless I constantly reflect on (and remain in) the love of Christ for myself" (Hendriksen, *New Testament Commentary,* Baker). He has called us to love one another.

—A. Koshy Muthalaly.

PRACTICAL POINTS

1. When we remain in Jesus, we will produce much fruit (John 15:1-4).
2. True disciples bear fruit and bring glory to God (vss. 5-8).
3. We are called to stay close to Jesus in obedience and love (vss. 9-11).
4. Joy comes when we love and obey Jesus.
5. We are called to love others as Jesus loved us and to show it through total sacrifice (vss. 12-13).
6. Obedience to our Lord Jesus marks us as His friends (vss. 14-15).
7. Jesus has appointed us to go out and bear fruit that will last (vs. 16a).
8. We now have the power to ask in the name of Jesus because we love Him, and our requests will be granted (vss. 16b-17).

—A. Koshy Muthalaly.

FOR DAILY MEDITATION

MONDAY, May 15.   Isa. 5:1-7.

The parable of the vineyard. The Lord had done everything possible to assure that His vineyard, Israel, would thrive and flourish, producing a bountiful harvest of sweet, juicy grapes. The Hebrew word translated "wild grapes" means "stinking, worthless things." Israel would be destroyed by the nations around her. The Lord had expected sweet grapes of justice and compassion from her, but she produced only foul-smelling, poisonous berries of oppression and anguished cries of those afflicted.

TUESDAY, May 16.   Isa. 27:2-6.

The Lord's vineyard. In contrast to the prophecy of judgment in Isaiah 2, this prophecy looks far beyond Israel's judgment and captivity to the time when Messiah would fulfill all that Israel was meant to be. The promise to Abraham would be realized as the gospel would go forth to bless all the nations of the world, bringing the righteousness of Christ by faith to every soul who would receive it.

WEDNESDAY, May 17.
Col. 2:6-10.

Rooted in Christ. In Christ, the Word of God, we have all we need. Anything we encounter from the world that does not align with God's Word is a potential trap to lead us away from God's will for our lives. Paul's warning echoes that of Peter: "Be sober, be vigilant; because your adversary the devil, as a roaring lion, walketh about, seeking whom he may devour" (I Pet. 5:8).

THURSDAY, May 18.
Ezek. 15:1-8.

A fruitless vine. What is a fruitless vine worth? In Ezekiel's day, Jerusalem had become a fruitless vine. Justice demanded that it be cut out by its roots and burned with fire. There comes a point when God's holiness demands that He set His face sternly against those who live faithlessly toward Him.

FRIDAY, May 19.   Ps. 80:8-19.

A vine out of Egypt. This psalm is a plea for restoration after judgment. As Ezekiel prophesied in yesterday's text, God had exposed His vineyard to hostile forces, which had laid it waste and left it desolate. The psalmist now pleads humbly for the Lord to restore His chastened people to His favor. God's chastening is often much more painful and costly than we imagine. But repentance and restoration are always available to those who earnestly and humbly seek Him.

SATURDAY, May 20.   Zech. 3:6-10.

My Servant the Branch. Zechariah's vision is an answer to yesterday's plea for Israel's restoration. Joshua was the high priest who returned to Jerusalem with the first exiles. The Lord made a solemn vow to Joshua that if he would be faithful, He would grant him authority over the people and access to His presence on their behalf. The Lord also prophesied of the Messiah, the Branch, who would one day make full atonement for Israel's sins, bringing peace to all those who are Abraham's true children by faith.

SUNDAY, May 21.   John 15:1-17.

Abide in Me. What does it mean to abide in Christ? Jesus said, "If ye keep my commandments, ye shall abide in my love; even as I have kept my Father's commandments, and abide in his love" (vs. 10). And what commandment does He give us? "This is my commandment, That ye love one another, as I have loved you" (vs. 12).
—*John Lody.*

SCRIPTURE LESSON TEXT

JOHN 17:6 I have manifested thy name unto the men which thou gavest me out of the world: thine they were, and thou gavest them me; and they have kept thy word.

7 Now they have known that all things whatsoever thou hast given me are of thee.

8 For I have given unto them the words which thou gavest me; and they have received *them,* and have known surely that I came out from thee, and they have believed that thou didst send me.

9 I pray for them: I pray not for the world, but for them which thou hast given me; for they are thine.

10 And all mine are thine, and thine are mine; and I am glorified in them.

11 And now I am no more in the world, but these are in the world, and I come to thee. Holy Father, keep through thine own name those whom thou hast given me, that they may be one, as we *are.*

12 While I was with them in the world, I kept them in thy name: those that thou gavest me I have kept, and none of them is lost, but the son of perdition; that the scripture might be fulfilled.

13 And now come I to thee; and these things I speak in the world, that they might have my joy fulfilled in themselves.

14 I have given them thy word; and the world hath hated them, because they are not of the world, even as I am not of the world.

15 I pray not that thou shouldest take them out of the world, but that thou shouldest keep them from the evil.

16 They are not of the world, even as I am not of the world.

17 Sanctify them through thy truth: thy word is truth.

18 As thou hast sent me into the world, even so have I also sent them into the world.

19 And for their sakes I sanctify myself, that they also might be sanctified through the truth.

20 Neither pray I for these alone, but for them also which shall believe on me through their word;

21 That they all may be one; as thou, Father, *art* in me, and I in thee, that they also may be one in us: that the world may believe that thou hast sent me.

NOTES

Jesus Prays for Believers

Lesson Text: John 17:6-21

Related Scriptures: Luke 22:31-32; John 17:22-24; Hebrews 7:24-27

TIME: A.D. 30   PLACE: Jerusalem

GOLDEN TEXT—"[I pray] that they all may be one; as thou, Father, art in me, and I in thee, that they also may be one in us: that the world may believe that thou hast sent me" (John 17:21).

Lesson Exposition

FAITH OF THE DISCIPLES—
John 17:6-8

Faith in God's Word (John 17:6). Christ disclosed who God the Father was to the disciples so that they would know what God is like (1:14, 18).

The disciples were an irrevocable gift from the Father to the Son. The Father had taken them out of the world. The unsaved are connected with the world, being separated from God and under His judgment (cf. John 3:16; Rom. 3:19). Satan controls and dominates them (II Cor. 4:4; I John 5:19).

The disciples belonged to the Father before He gave them to the Son (John 6:37, 39, 44). They placed their faith in Him as the Christ (6:68-69). Their faith was evidenced through their continued obedience to God's Word.

Faith in Christ (John 17:7-8). The disciples knew the words of truth, which Christ gave them, were from the Father (8:28; 12:49). As a result, the disciples were convinced that Christ had been sent from the Father (5:36).

REQUESTS FOR THE DISCIPLES—
John 17:9-19

Special prayer (John 17:9-10). Jesus' concern for His disciples prompted Him to pray for them in particular. It would be later that He would pray for those who would trust in Him because of the disciples' witness (vs. 20). Jesus interceded for His disciples, for they were under His special care. Though given to Him, they still belonged to the Father.

Kept from defection (John 17:11-12). Jesus prayed for His disciples because He was no more in the world. He anticipated His death, resurrection, and ultimate return to the Father (14:1-2). Christ was concerned for the spiritual well-being of the disciples, for they would remain in the world.

Jesus prayed that the Father would keep the disciples through His name. Christ was praying that the disciples would be guarded from abandoning their faith by the Father's omnipotent power.

Jesus prayed that the disciples would be united together as one, just as He and the Father are one. Their unity was demonstrated through their common love for Christ and for one another.

While Jesus was with the disciples, He safely guarded them in the power of the Father's name. He kept them from defecting from the faith. Not one of them was "lost" (17:12), referring to eternal spiritual ruin (cf. II Pet. 3:9). The only exception was "the son of perdition" (John 17:12).

As the "son of perdition," Judas made his decision to betray Christ, for which he was fully accountable (Matt. 26:24). His defection was in fulfillment of the Scripture. Peter explained that in Acts 1:16, 20 as he referred to Judas's failure. His statements were drawn from Psalms 69:25 and 109:8.

Experiencing Christ's joy (John 17:13-14). Jesus had spoken the truth to His disciples while He was with them. He found joy in His obedience to the Father's will (15:10-11). He desired that the disciples would follow His example of obedience and experience the same joy He did.

The disciples were not of the world, even as Christ is not. This radical contrast would draw hatred from the world (vss. 18-19). The world is intolerant of the truth because it is contrary to its views and values. The disciples stood with Christ, which resulted in their facing the same intolerant rejection He experienced.

Protection from the devil (John 17:15-16). Jesus was not praying that the Father would remove the disciples from the world. Though they lived in an antagonistic and perilous environment, the disciples had a mission to fulfill.

Christ asked for protection for them from "the evil" (vs. 15), which refers to "the evil one," the devil (cf. I John 2:13-14; 5:18). Satan is behind much of the corrupting influences of the world.

Sanctification by the truth (John 17:17-19). Christ prayed that the Father would "sanctify," meaning set apart, the disciples by the truth. He desired that their thoughts, words, and actions be in complete conformity to God's truth.

WITNESS OF THE DISCIPLES— John 17:20-21

Jesus expanded His prayer to include those who would be saved through the witness of the disciples. Christ prayed that all believers, including those not yet born, would be united as one. The oneness of all believers is rooted in the unity that exists between the Father and the Son (10:30, 38). It is a spiritual unity of love, mind, heart, and purpose (13:34-35). The message of the disciples would be a credible witness to the world.

—*Jack Riggs.*

PRACTICAL POINTS

1. When we read Jesus' teachings, we are learning God's very Word (John 17:6-8).

2. Believers belong to both the Father and the Son, who provide for their spiritual welfare (vss. 9-10).

3. Those who act in opposition to God's salvation bring eternal doom upon themselves (vss. 11-12).

4. Believers can be what God desires of them while living in the world (vss. 13-17).

5. Christ has sent us into a hostile world to be His witnesses (vss. 18-19).

6. Christ prayed for those of us who are His followers today (vs. 20).

7. Believers should seek to be united in truth, love, and purpose to glorify Christ (vs. 21).

—*Jack Riggs.*

FOR DAILY MEDITATION

MONDAY, May 22.   Heb. 7:24-27.

Our High Priest and Intercessor. Because Christ lives forever, His priesthood is forever. Because His priesthood is eternal, those who come to God through Him are saved. Jesus will continue to make intercession for you for all eternity, and His pleas are effectual because His sacrifice of Himself was sufficient for every sin forever.

TUESDAY, May 23.   John 17:22-26.

Jesus prays for our oneness with God. If the church's perfect unity is how the world is meant to know that God the Father sent Jesus (cf. vs. 23), then we are doing a really lousy job of it! All the world sees in us is division and strife over what seem to them the most trivial of matters. Be thankful that somehow, despite our enormous failures in the area of unity, God continues to draw people to Himself through the power of His gospel. Pray and strive for genuine unity today (cf. Eph. 4:1-3).

WEDNESDAY, May 24.
Luke 22:24-34.

The Lord prays for Peter's faith. It was the evening of the night of Jesus' betrayal, but His disciples were wrangling about which of them was the greatest. So, Jesus told them that if they really wanted to be great in His kingdom, they should strive to be humble and subservient to one another. Jesus prayed especially for Peter, who boasted that he was ready to follow Jesus to prison and death. But that very night, he denied three times even knowing Jesus. Jesus' prayers were answered, of course; Peter eventually became the rock Jesus intended him to be.

THURSDAY, May 25.
Rom. 10:5-17.

Believe and confess Jesus is Lord. Paul took his missionary enterprises very seriously. He realized that in order to believe, people need the gospel preached to them. To hear it preached, churches must send out preachers. Pray earnestly today that the Lord will send workers into His harvest (cf. Matt. 9:37-38).

FRIDAY, May 26.   Isa. 61:1-11.

The Lord's favor. This is the passage that Jesus chose to read from in the synagogue at Nazareth, His hometown (Luke 4:16-32). After His reading, Jesus said, "This day is this scripture fulfilled in your ears" (vs. 21). Jesus was telling the Jews of Nazareth that Gentiles were more worthy of His miracles than they were. This sent them into a murderous fury toward Him!

SATURDAY, May 27.
I John 3:19-24.

Ask in confidence. Getting us to indulge in self-condemnation is a favorite tactic of Satan. Although we should rightly examine ourselves to verify the genuineness of our faith and love toward Christ (cf. II Cor. 13:5), even that can be twisted by the enemy of our souls. But God is the final Judge, and nothing is hidden from Him, including our hearts. He is always faithful to forgive those who are truly repentant.

SUNDAY, May 28.   John 17:6-21.

Prayer for protection. Jesus is the Word of God. The Scriptures are also the Word of God. Jesus is the truth. The Scriptures are also the truth. Jesus makes us holy. The Scriptures also make us holy. Jesus prayed that the Father would protect us from the devil. The Scriptures are our sword that the Holy Spirit uses to fight off the temptations that Satan brings to us. If we resist him, he will flee (cf. Jas. 4:7).
—*John Lody.*

PARAGRAPHS ON PLACES AND PEOPLE

TREASURY (OF THE TEMPLE)

As the book of Joshua makes clear, Israel needed a place where they could store their treasures dedicated to God (cf. 6:19, 24). David's instructions to Solomon for the temple included a treasury (I Chr. 28:12). Solomon's temple contained a place for storing the gold and silver that was dedicated to the Lord (I Kgs. 5:17). In the time of Jesus, the priests served as administrators of the treasures in the temple.

The exact location of the temple treasury has been disputed, but because women had access to giving offerings, it is thought to have been located by the Court of the Women, which was located in the outer court, past the Beautiful Gate. There were boxes, with openings shaped like inverted megaphones, that were positioned to receive the donations of the worshippers. Jesus saw the widow give her two mites there (Mark 12:41).

JESUS' TOMB

For centuries, emperors, kings, historians, archaeologists, and filmmakers have searched for the location of Jesus' temporary tomb. Most Bible scholars will caution that there is not enough proof of its exact location.

Two locations are the main contenders. The first contender is the Garden Tomb, also known as Gordon's Tomb, named after Charles Gordon, who discovered a tomb two-hundred-and-seventy-five yards outside Jerusalem, in a garden, near a rock formation that looked like a skull (supposedly Golgotha).

The second, and strongest, contender is the tomb in the Church of the Holy Sepulchre. In 325 A.D., Emperor Constantine sent a group to find the tomb. They followed local tradition that it was under a temple built by Emperor Hadrian in the second century. When they leveled the temple, they found a tomb underneath. They then built a shrine around it. Scholars verify that the tomb existed in the first century, but no one can say with certainty that Jesus rested there. Located in the Christian Quarter of the Old City, the site draws many visitors yearly.

ALL THAT ARE IN THE GRAVES

Jesus referred to the resurrection of the righteous and the unrighteous that would take place in the last day. Both will physically rise from their graves to stand before God, who will determine their eternal destinies. Christ's perfect work on the cross gives Him the authority to raise the dead to life. Those who have put their trust in Him will live for eternity in heaven.

ALL THOSE WHO CAME BEFORE ME

Jesus' statement in John 10:8 that all who came before Him were thieves and robbers must be taken within the context of His being the door of the sheepfold. He was not referring to Old Testament prophets, because none of them claimed to be the Messiah, and they all pointed to Him.

Jesus was talking about those who pretended to be the means by which all others could come to God. They claimed to be the mediators between man and God.

—Don Ruff.

FOR COMFORT AND CHALLENGE

RUTH MARIE REVECKY

It's Springtime!

Springtime is a surge of energy that bursts forth eternally. It gives us comfort to see new life emerging all around us.

Springtime dresses trees and shrubs in shades of green and brings forth colorful flowers that create radiant bouquets.

Birds fly hither and yon, building nests in which to hatch their young.

Fill your thoughts with happy times, remembering those pleasant and joyous moments.

Keep springtime in your daily life, and share a smile with a friend.

Daily Prayers

Be sure to begin each day by saying your daily prayers; do not forget to say thank You, God, for a safe journey throughout the night.

Peaceful sleep is a gift from God, giving us strength for each new day. Courage comes from God, for He really cares about you.

Say thank You, God, before each meal, for He will surely supply your every need.

Say prayers for people in foreign lands and for your family and friends.

God Is Forever Faithful

Tears can flow from joy as well as from sorrow; but whatever the occasion may be, God is near to comfort you.

God is forever faithful; He wipes away our tears of sorrow and rejoices in our tears of laughter.

God is always faithful, giving us strength for our everyday challenges.

God does hear our daily prayers and petitions. God is and always will be forever faithful.

Meeting Daily Challenges

When you are in the autumn of your life and there is a steep hill to climb, be sure to mix a full cup of faith with a heaping measure of patience.

Pray for courage. Before you know it, peace and strength will flow inside you; and even though you move more slowly, your daily challenges may seem less stressful.

Daily prayer and meditation will give you comfort and help sustain you.